what time is it?

stories about painting, shadows & the sun

ISBN: 978-2-36568-070-7

franck leibovici

what time is it?

stories about painting, shadows & the sun

JBE BOOKS

for a more precise and accurate history of passing time.

there was an investigative journalism website that would tell you what time a photograph was taken when its metadata had been deleted. the website would, for instance, use a picture showing syrian generals standing on the side of a mountain, looking intensely at something happening outside the frame. the author of that article would nimbly jump from *google street view*, to localize the group of men, to another website allowing them to calculate, among other things, the path of the sun. that website could deduce from the position and length of the shadows in the picture the exact time when the photograph had been taken. i was amazed by such a clever yet simple process of investigation: using everyday life knowledge and simple gestures—looking at the sun to know what time it is—the author would actually achieve *osint* (open-source intelligence) operations. armed with the location, the date, and the hour, they would then be able to easily demonstrate that if kurdish villages had been under a (probably chemical) attack on that very day, in that very place down that very mountain side, these syrian generals were undoubtedly watching it from above, making sure the military operations were carried out smoothly.

i started daydreaming about using the same tools elsewhere, applying them to other—less tragic but equally relevant—materials and situations. soon enough, i felt strongly that a history of painting written through timestamped scenes would definitely be enlightening. looking at this or that painting, we would finally know *precisely* where and when the depicted scene had taken place, when nothing, until then, would ever tell us anything about that in the painting's label. everything—from the most innocuous pastoral scenes to depictions of crowded boulevards, even including the most intimate portraits—could finally be assigned to a time and a place, and the metadata be renewed.

evidently, the scene would have to be taking place outside, as artificial lighting would skew the calculations around the shadows. yet other possibilities quickly arose: the mere examination of what the sun was tracing on the ground might finally reveal when exactly eve took a bite of the apple, when exactly jesus or his mother, mary, ascended to heaven, when exactly, in heaven or in hell, the battle between angels and demons *really* did take place.

the endeavor was shaping up nicely: an *informed* history of painting, which wouldn't have to look past the canvas to find relevant data and knowledge. no more uncertainty, no more conjecturing. after centuries of more or less antagonistic arguments, finally there would be a simultaneously internalist and factual history.

a lockdown imposed by a pandemic offered me time to look up the *google cultural institute*: for some years now, *google* has been collaborating with hundreds of museums to put their permanent collections online. i would only have to search the database for "light and shadow" to harvest instantly hundreds, if not thousands, of paintings featuring those characteristics.

i soon realized, however, that many sections and areas of the global history of painting would remain out of reach, defying any commitment to exactitude: asian silk painting knows no shadows, and neither do persian miniatures, pictograms in pre-columbian codices, aboriginal drawings in australian caves, parietal art, icons from the european middle ages, or more recently the 20th century's abstract modern painting. in the end, i could only rely on the four or five past centuries—a relatively short period in history when *realism* would manifest as a goal.

the scope of my plan was shrinking, granted, but i could still envision a book, a very simple book, a children's book, which would journey through the history of painting—western painting, let's admit it—with one simple question in mind, "what time is it?" teaching kids how to read the time through paintings: pedagogy in action!

but, soon enough, yet again, some new pitfalls...

of course, it would be very easy to claim that painting doesn't have to be realistic, that assigning scenes to examination as if they were summoned at the police station would negate the whole concept of art, that my questions overall are futile and useless, if not dangerous. all right, sure. but still... it is always useful to ask questions that needn't be asked at all.

the following pages tell the story of that struggling, in order to know, in spite of everything, what time it is. the whole world was in lockdown. while we would wait for this pandemic to end, what else was there to do but count the hours while looking at paintings?

p.s.: obviously, i might have made some mistakes in my hypotheses and assessment regarding the shadows. readers are more than welcome to redo the math and check my calculations, using the same tools, and therefore contribute as well to a more precise and accurate history of passing time.

"...the origin of the art of painting is uncertain
...the egyptians claim that it was invented among themselves
six thousand years ago before it passed over into greece. as to the greeks,
they say it was discovered at sicyon or corinth.
all agree that it was born out of tracing an outline round a human's shadow..."
pliny the elder, *natural history*

"in my properties, everything is flat, nothing moves,
and if there are shapes here and there,
then where is the light coming from? never a shadow."
henri michaux, *my properties*

"what is the purpose of the shadow in a painting,
if not to indicate the time?"
david hockney in *le monde*

"in more than one other [watercolor], the vast landscape (in which the mythical scene, the fabulous heroes occupy a tiny place and seem almost lost) is rendered, from the mountaintops to the sea, with an exactitude which, rather than just the hour, tells the time down to the very minute thanks to the precise angle of the declining sun, to the fleeting fidelity of the shadows. in this way, the artist confers, by instantaneizing it, a sense of historical, experienced reality to the symbol of the fable, paints it and relates it to a definite point in the past."

marcel proust, *the guermantes way*

"the trees have become nothing but dots constructing shadows."

claude royet-journoud, *the use and attributes of the heart*

in praise of shadows

jun'ichirō tanizaki

i never knew what time it was

david antin

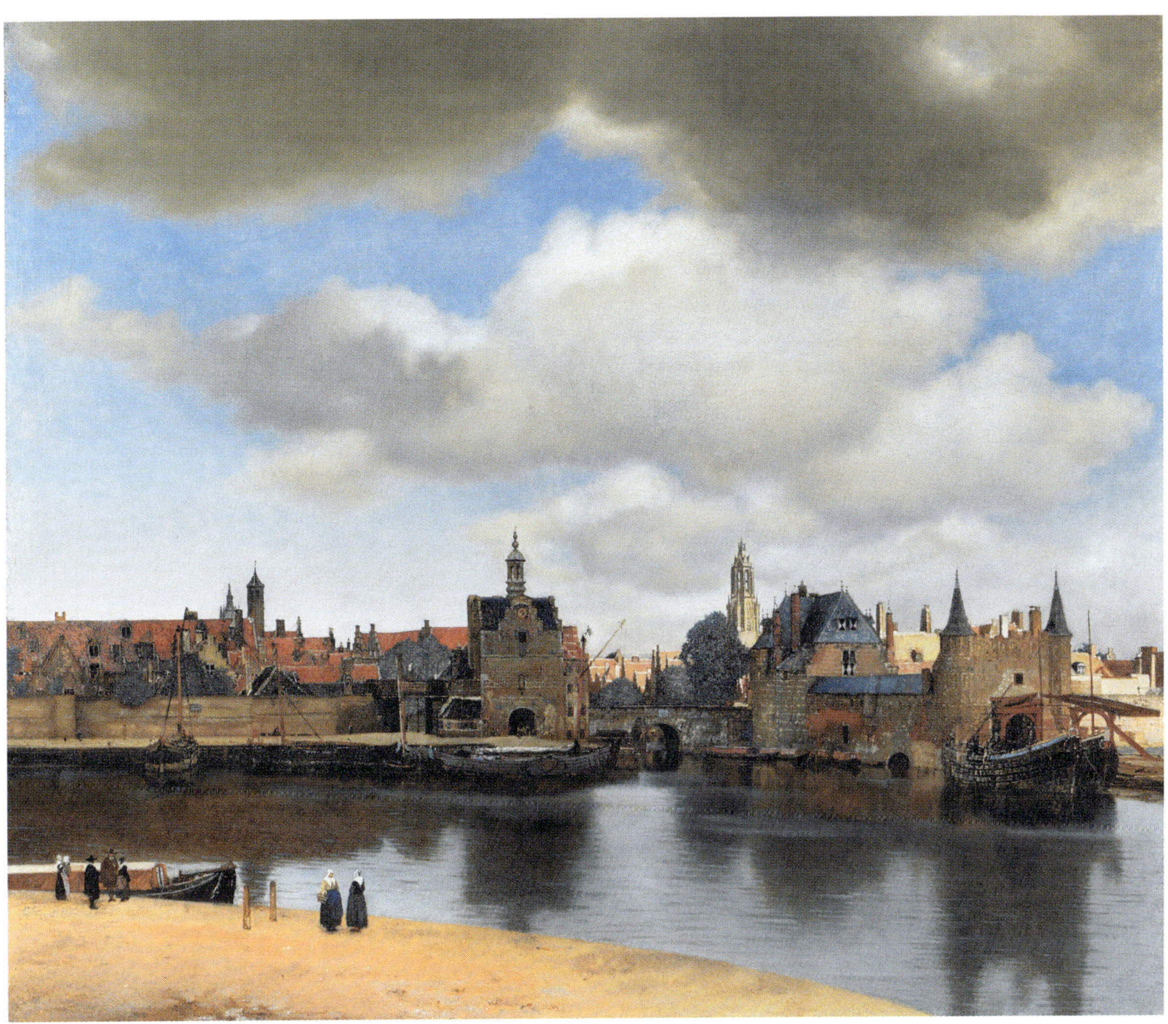

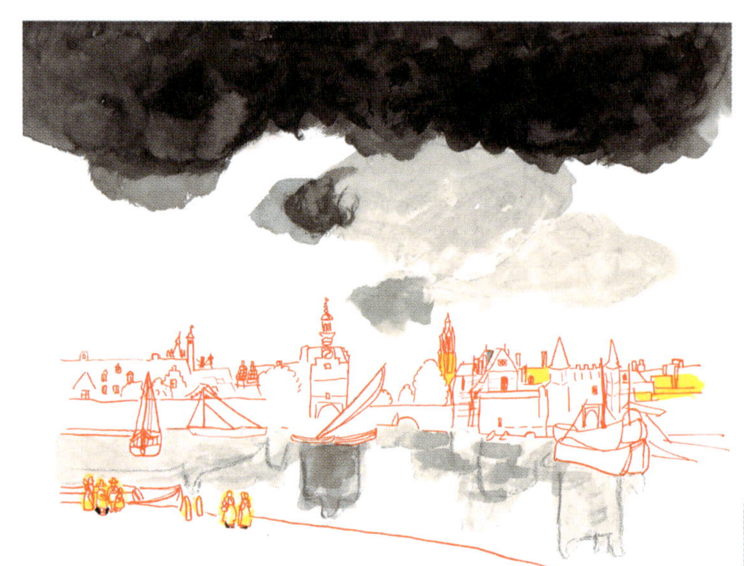

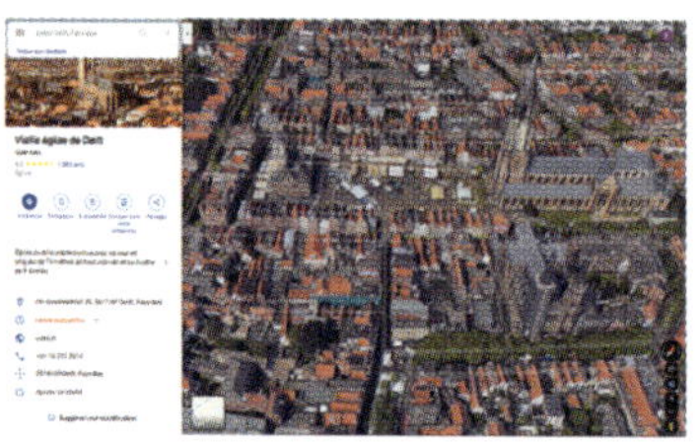

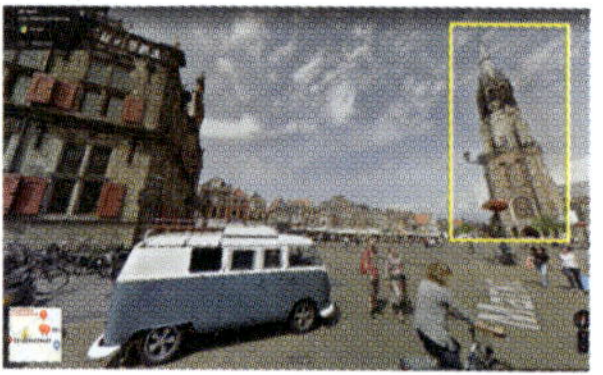

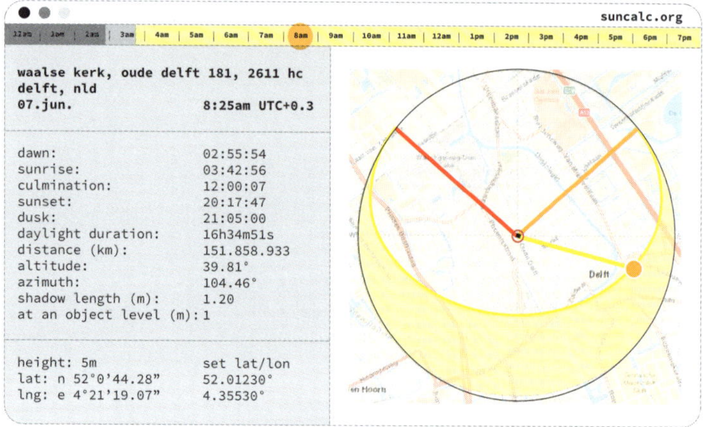

johannes vermeer, *view of delft*,
oil on canvas, 1659–1660, 96.5 × 115.7 cm

the view is facing north. the sun is in the east or the south-east. on the right side, sunbeams cast light on "the little patch of yellow wall" that bergotte and proust liked so much—actually, it is probably not a wall but a roof reflecting the sun—and, in the center of the painting, also illuminate the church steeple. despite the shadow one chimney casts in the opposite direction, it is early morning, around **8:25** a.m. the barges indicate that herring fishing season has started (may-june). the trees are in bloom, their foliage thick. the bell has been brought down for maintenance work (1660-1661). the reflection in the water is stretched to better connect the background to the foreground. an early morning of june 1660, then, in delft.

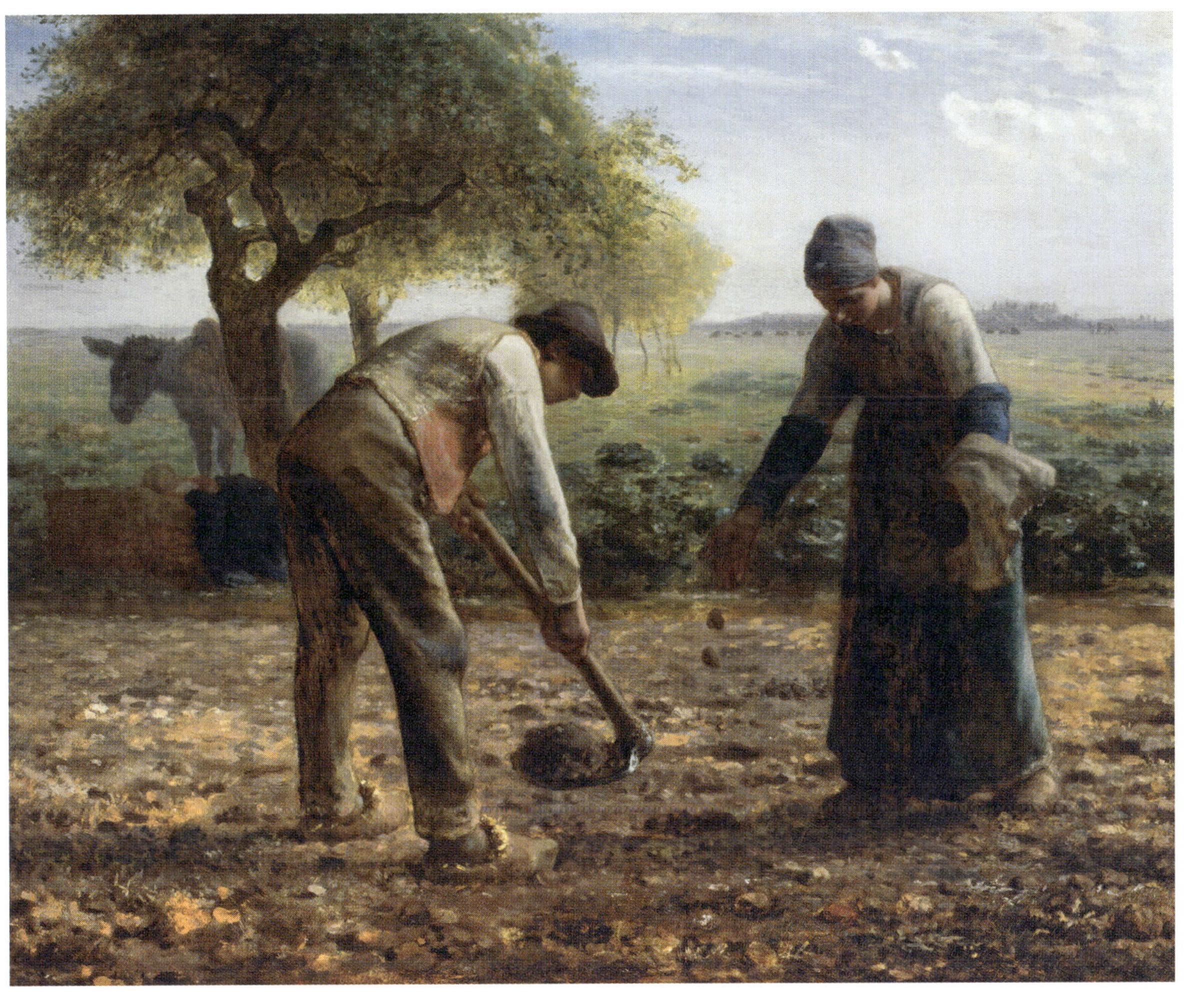

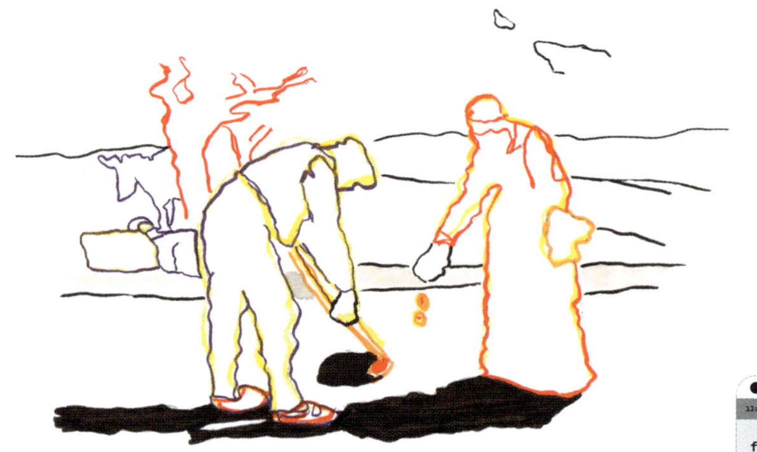

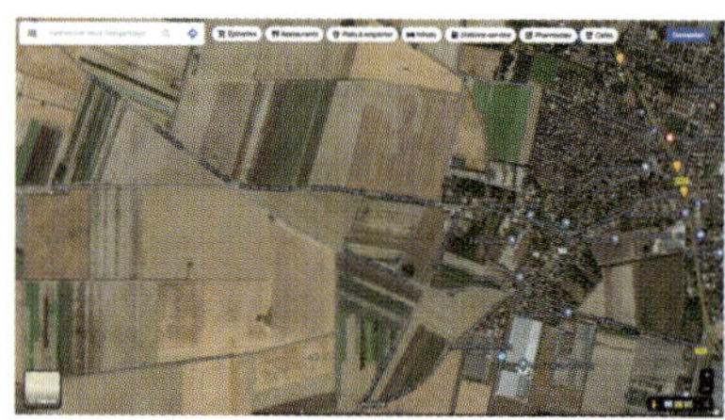

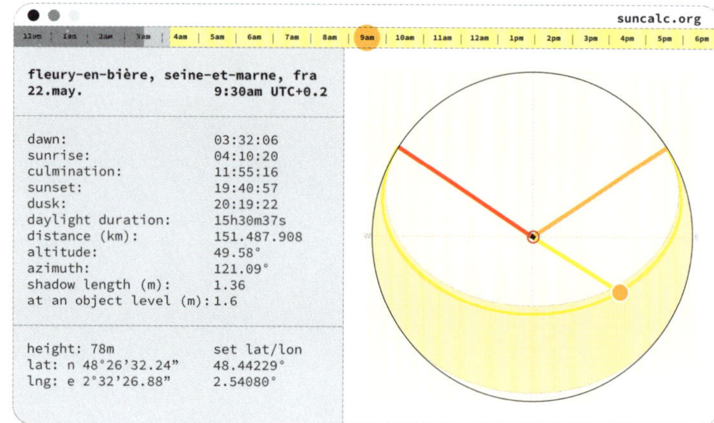

jean-françois millet, *potato planters*,
oil on canvas, c. 1861, 82.5 × 101.3 cm

these fields in the plains of barbizon are the same as in *the gleaners*. according to the website *gardeningknowhow.com*, potatoes should be planted in spring at the earliest, between the end of march and that of may, during the ascending moon. the technique depicted in this scene is "hilling."

the fruit trees mark former property lines. it's probably morning, and therefore the sun, on the right, is in the east (the donkey is facing north).

the angle of the shadows might indicate **6:45** a.m., but at this hour their lengths should be twice or thrice bigger than the height of the persons (3.73 meters [12.23 ft.] for a 1.60 meters [5.25 ft.] woman). suncalc.org tells us we have to wait until may 22 to get a shadow of 1.36 meters [4.46 ft.] for a 1.60 meters [5.25 ft.] woman—and not before **9:30** a.m., at best.

instead of deducing that peasants don't actually wake up that early, shouldn't we consider the possibility that jean-françois millet sketched them fairly late in the morning (he's the late riser)?

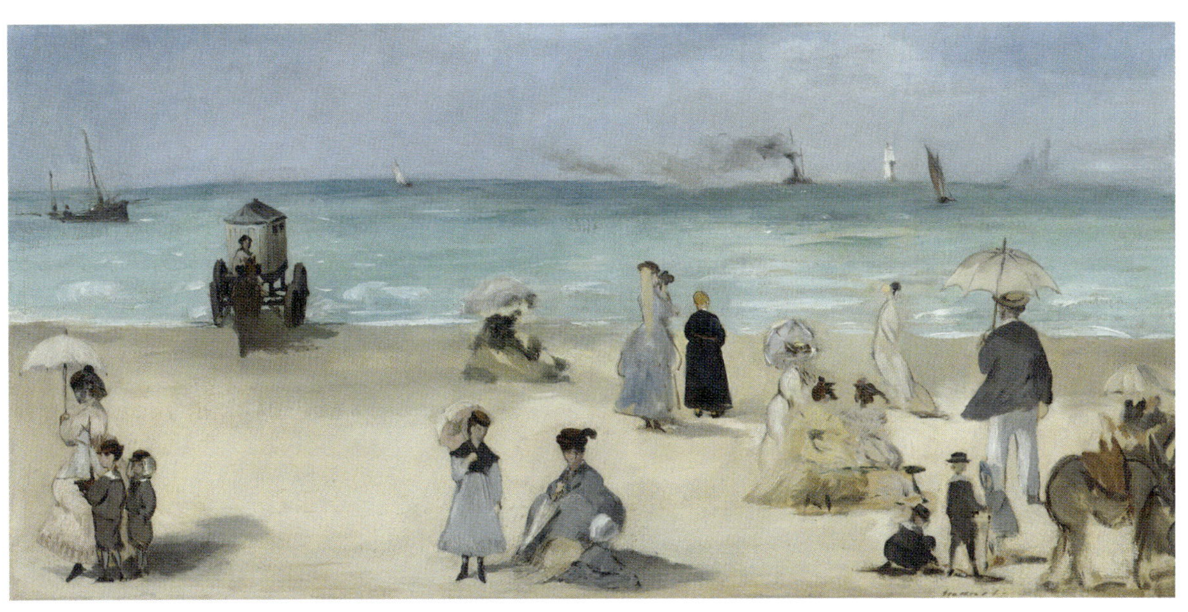

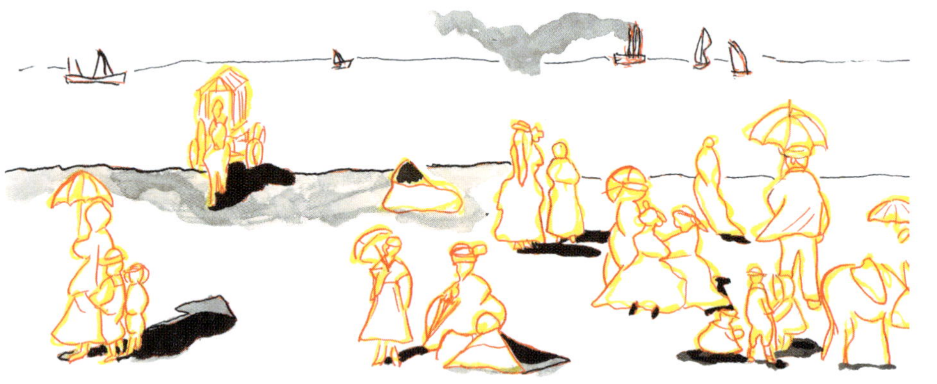

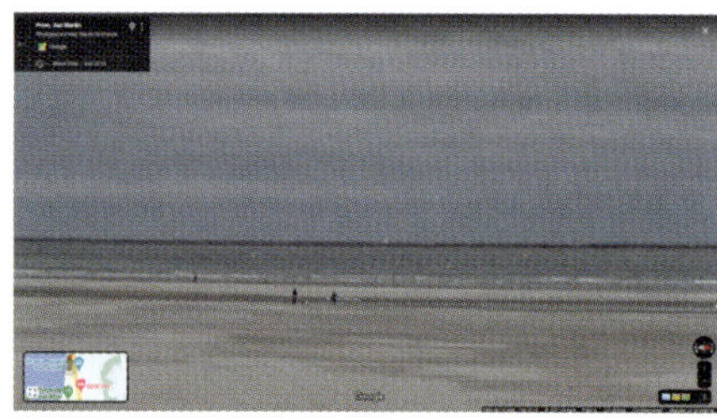

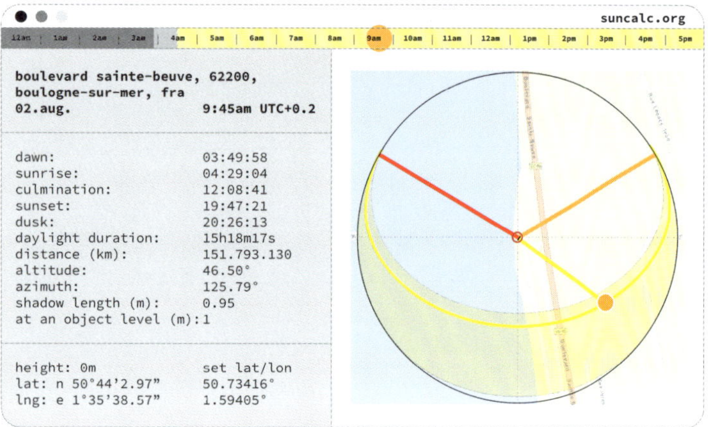

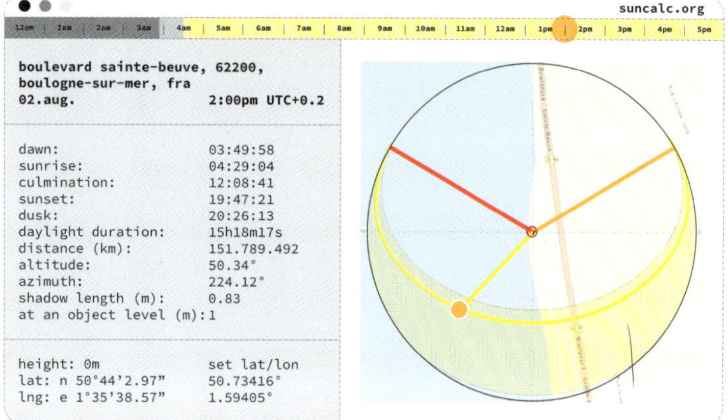

édouard manet, ***on the beach. boulogne-sur-mer,***
oil on canvas, 1868, 32 × 66 cm

summer 1868. since the construction of the famous sea wall called *digue carnot* wouldn't start before 1879, it's only logical that it isn't featured in this painting.

the horizon line marks the west. and yet, it is not easy to figure out what time it is: on the left of the painting, the woman holding an umbrella, flanked by two children, casts a shadow towards the sea, indicating that it is **9:45** a.m.

but the shadow of another character, the lady in the center with a long veil, holding something black—a flower bouquet, or binoculars?—points towards the north and the man wearing a boater, as if to indicate it is **2:00** p.m. (one of the hottest hours there are).

should we therefore look at this painting as an avant-gardist collage of sketches brought back in various notebooks to be stitched together leisurely, in the coolness of the studio? in that case, manet, influenced and inspired by traditional japanese art, would care even less about any kind of realism in depicting shadows. or should we rather read the painting from left to right, as if it was showing the slow passing of time? the canvas as film; the film within the painting?

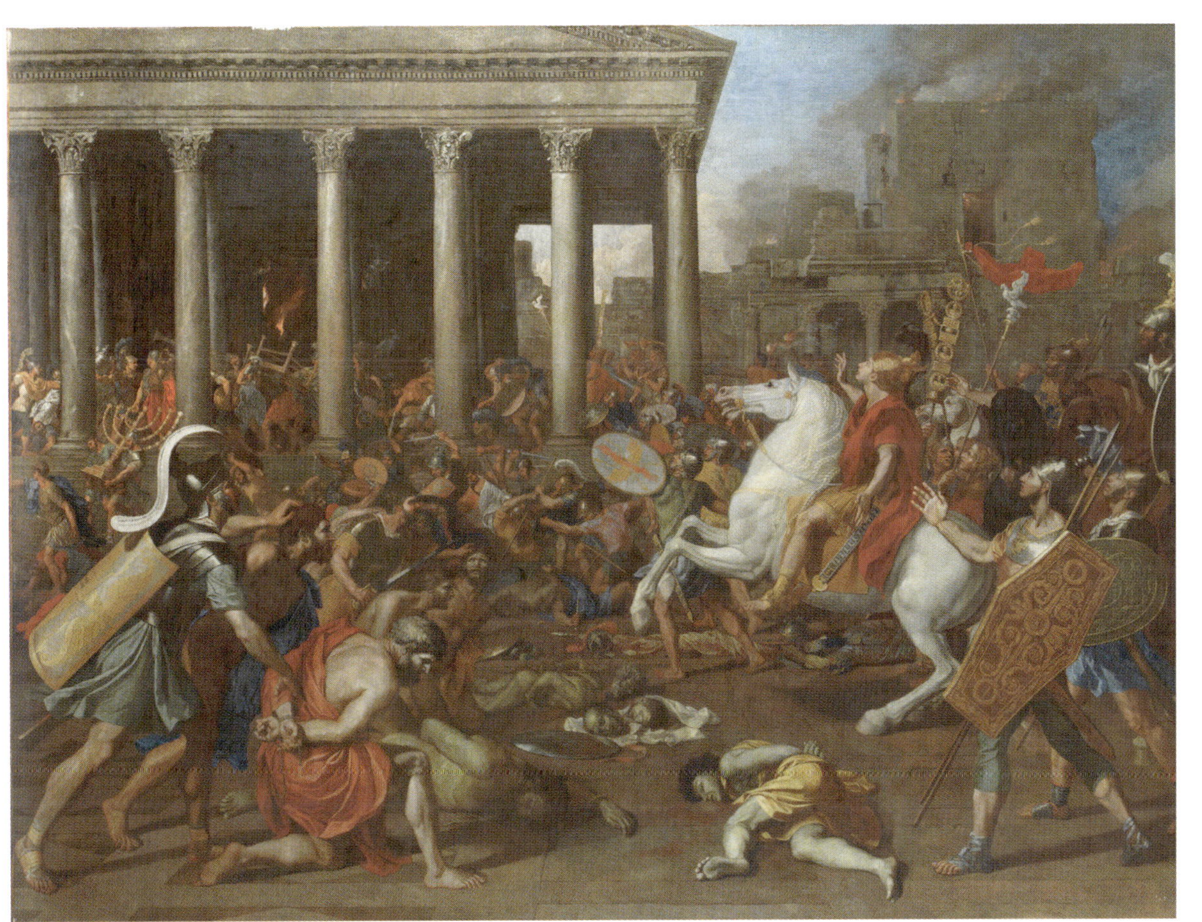

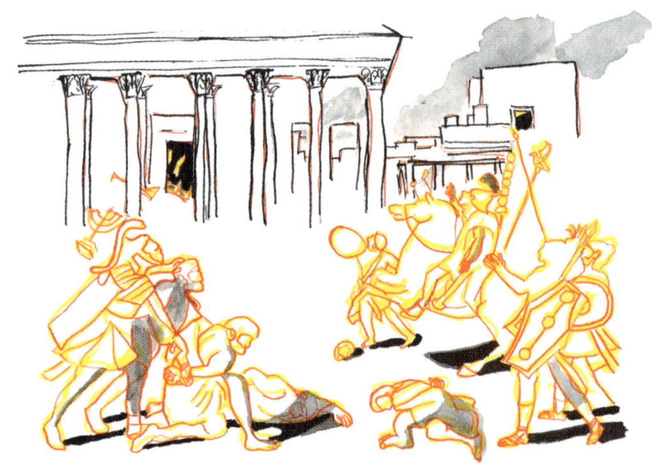

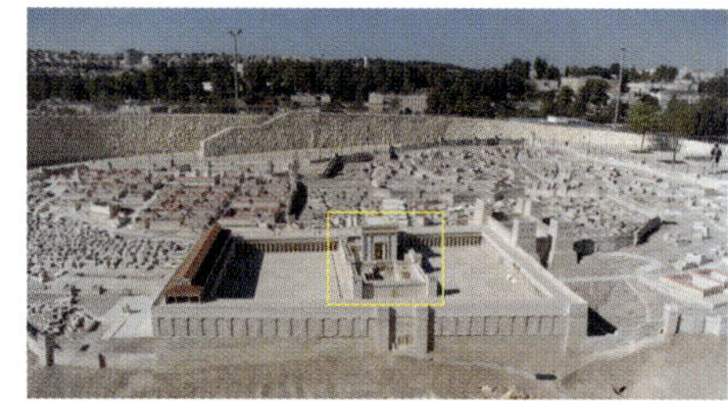

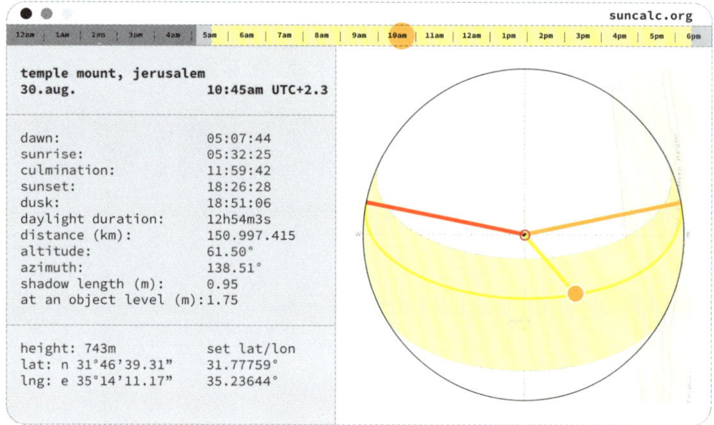

nicolas poussin, ***the conquest of jerusalem by emperor titus***,
oil on canvas, 1638, 148 × 199 cm

the painting's title designates the destruction of jerusalem's second temple. on the left, a soldier, faithfull to the future *bas-relief* that will praise the triumph of titus, carries away the famous seven-lamp *menorah*. the fire that another soldier started inside the temple—against titus' will, according to flavius josephus—is clearly visible.

however, not only do the massacred civilians not wear the kippah, but also, and above all, the columns of the temple look surprisingly greek: all the models recreating the temple concur in the absence of columns around the *holy of holies*. the only colonnades were lining the outside walls of the esplanade. but whatever way we consider the overall layout, in the painting the columns are undoubtedly in the middle of the esplanade. according to the hebrew calendar, the destruction of the temple took place on the *ninth of av*, i.e. august 30, 70 ce. the issue is the orientation of the temple's entrance. some place it in the east, so as to align it with the rising sun. the position of the shadows would therefore point towards **10:45** a.m. it is 10:45 a.m., but are we really in jerusalem?

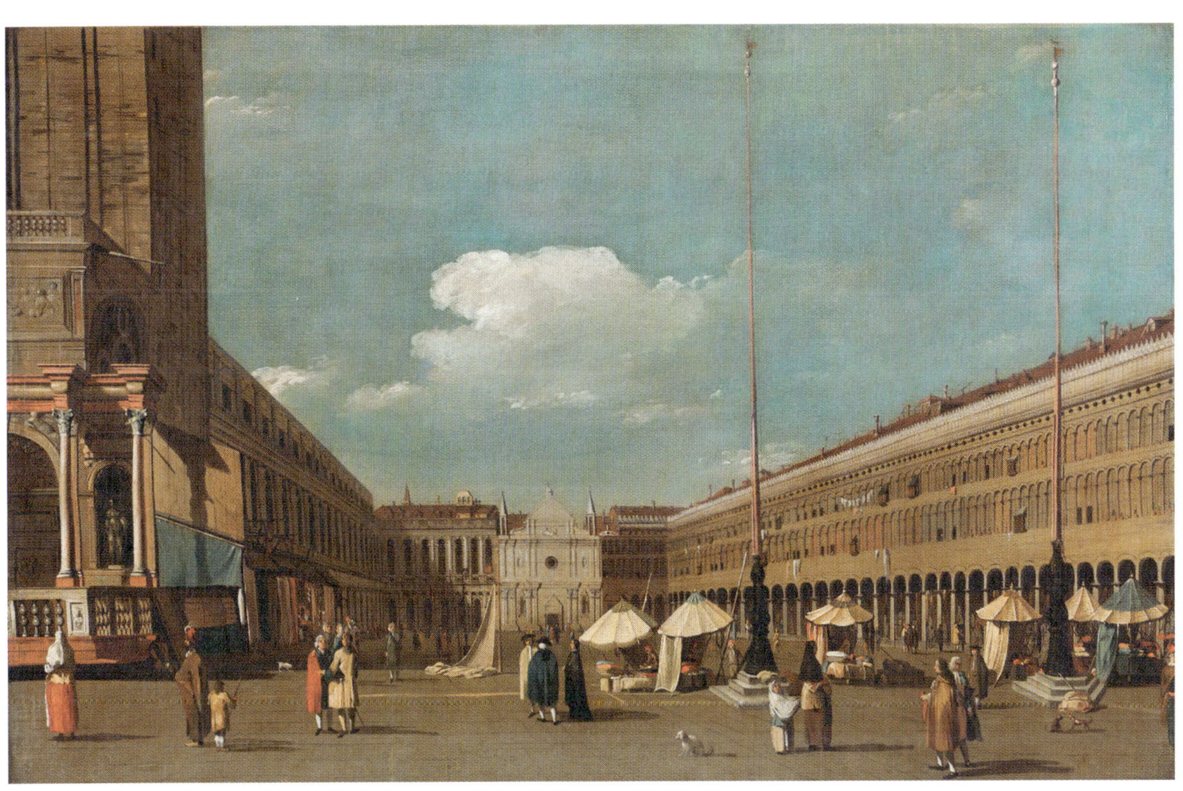

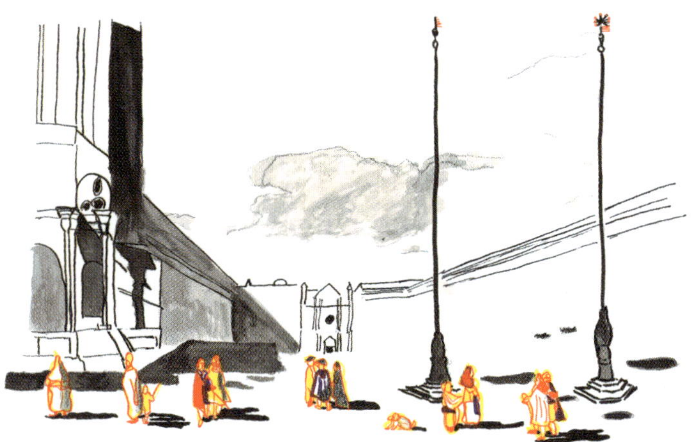

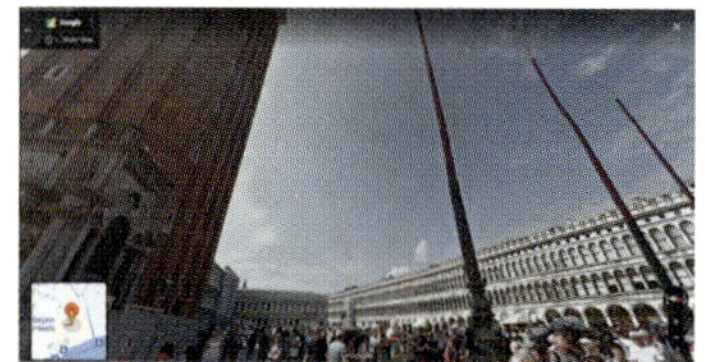

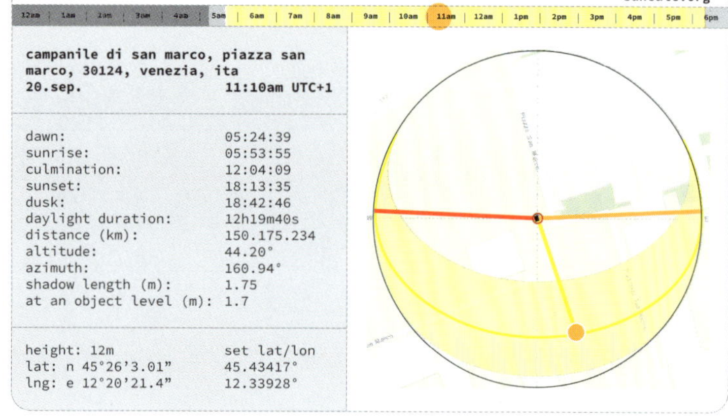

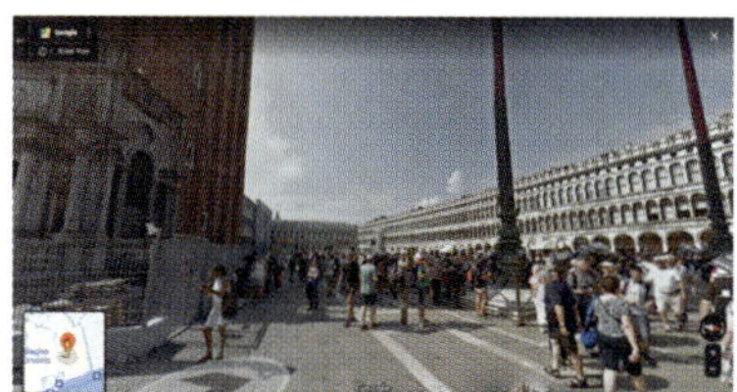

canaletto (giovanni antonio canal, known as),
piazza san marco, west view, south of the central line,
oil on canvas, 1750–1760, 72.4 × 113.2 cm

the columns of piazza san marco probably haven't grown taller in the past two or three centuries. nevertheless, the perpendicular shadows here indicate that it's close to noon (**11:10** a.m.), and their length, equal at this hour to the objects casting them, suggest that the date is close to that of september 20. the weather is nice; nothing foreshadows the *acqua alta* that occurred on october 9, 1750 (if the painting was created afterwards, the flood amounts to nothing but a faint memory).

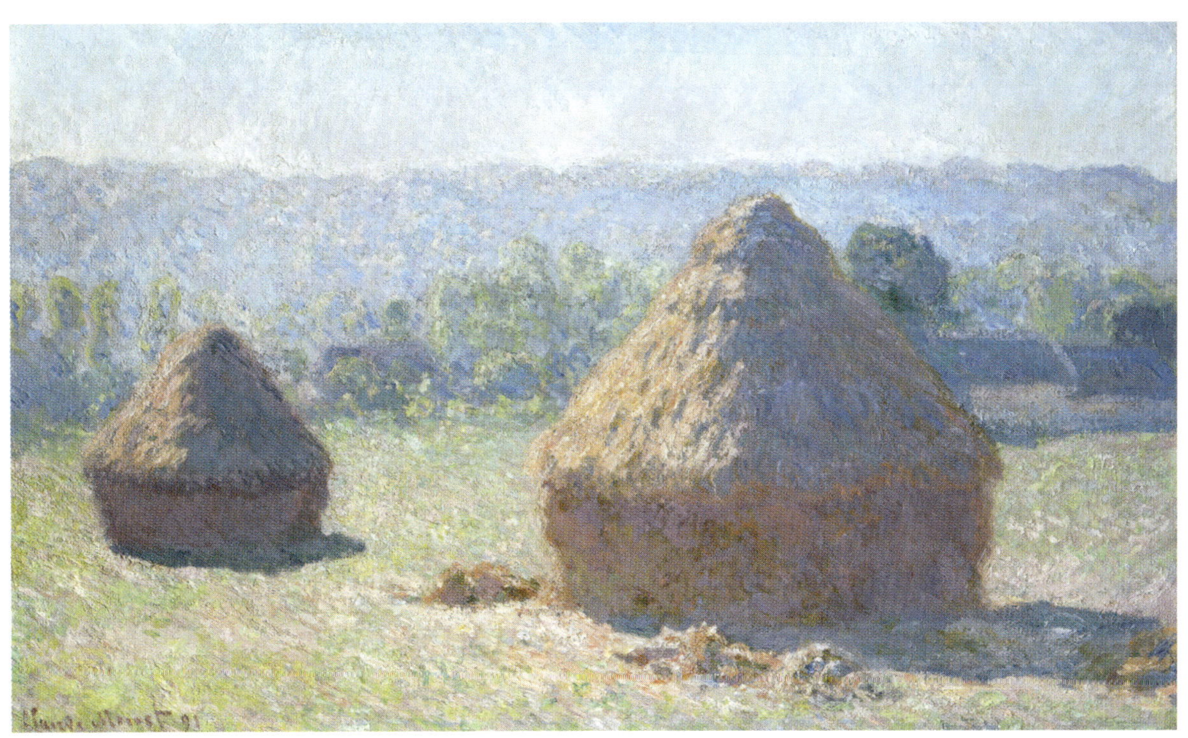

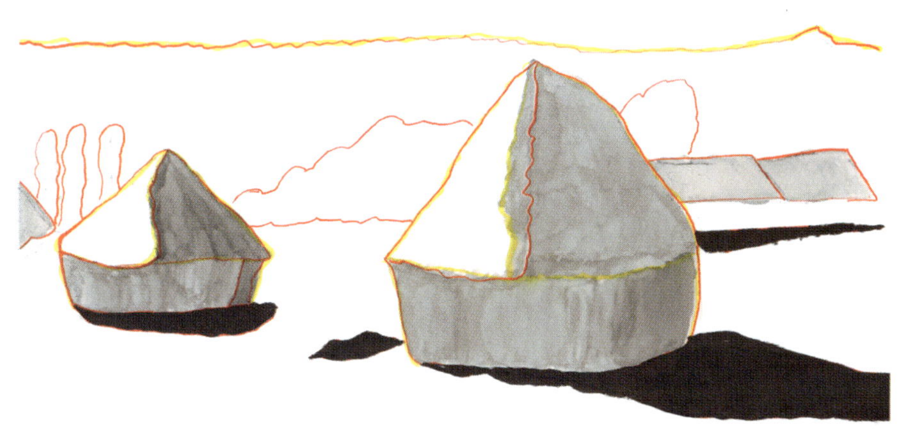

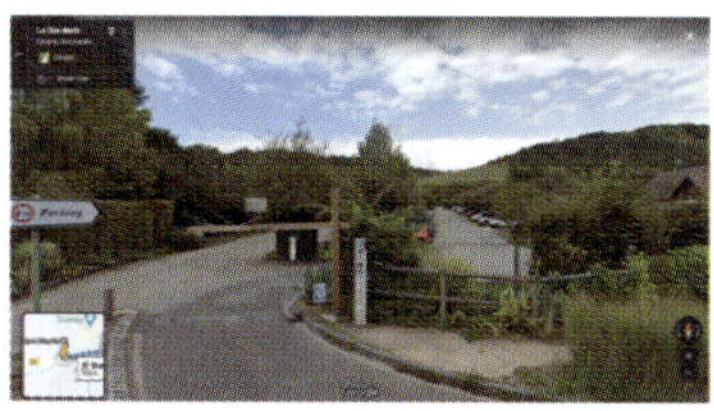

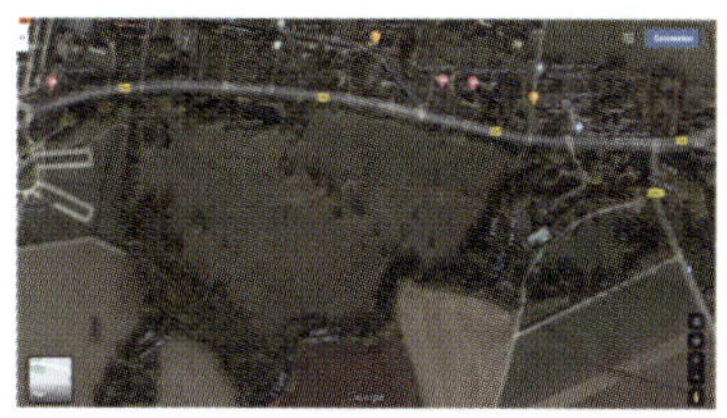

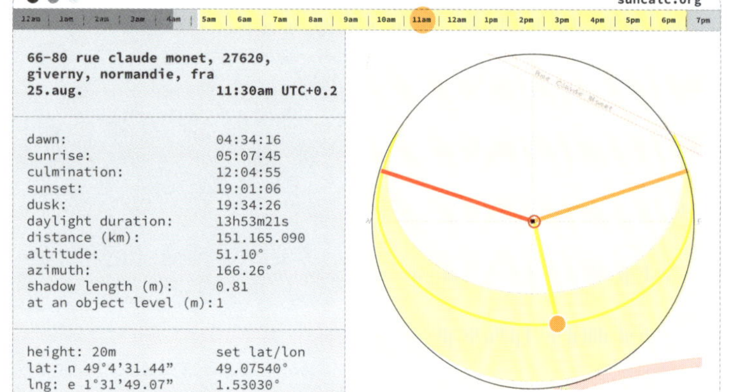

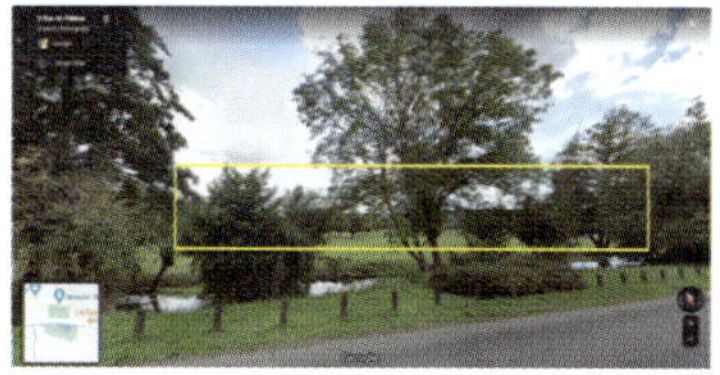

claude monet, ***haystacks, end of summer***,
oil on canvas, 1891, 60.5 × 100.8 cm

“giverny, le clos morin,” as legend has it. very well. but what’s the orientation? no landmark in the painting helps us assess it. only the orientation, however, could actually establish whether those shadows are from the morning or the afternoon sun.

google street view suggests that either the clos morin has changed a lot over the years (it is now a parking lot), or the haystacks were painted in another location. indeed, the mountains in the background form a much straighter horizon line than that of the actual clos morin. maybe we should wander a few minutes away from there and find a vast field which would feature similar hills in the south. the shadows point north-northwest, indicating that the sun is south-southeast. they are very short, shorter than the objects casting them. on august 25, in the late morning, around **11:30** a.m., a 2-meter [6.56 ft.] high haystack would cast a 1.60-meter [5.25 ft.] long shadow. it’s more than in july (the same shadow would then measure up to 1.20 meters [3.94 ft.]) but less than in september (it would go past 1.80 meters [5.90 ft.]).

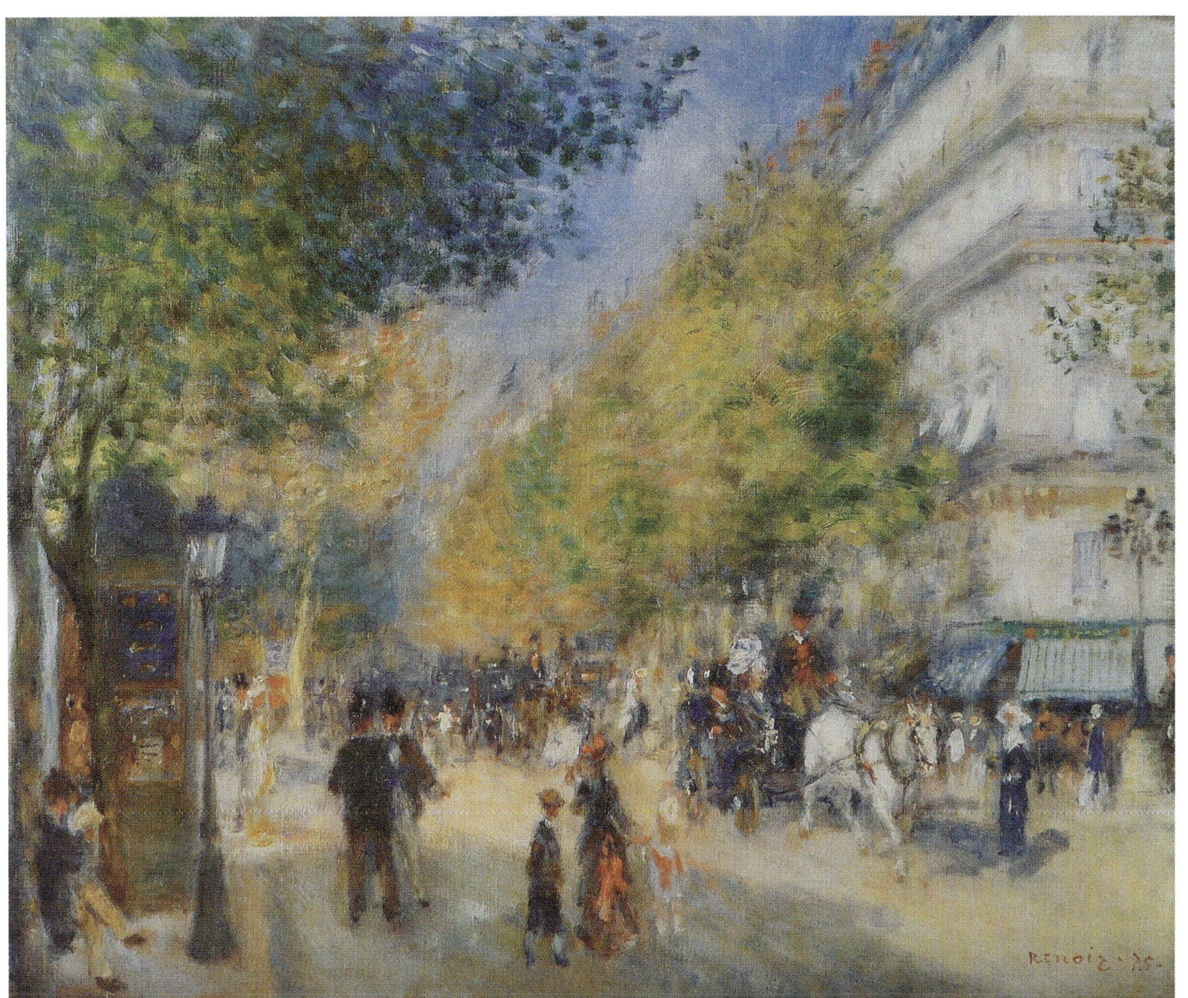

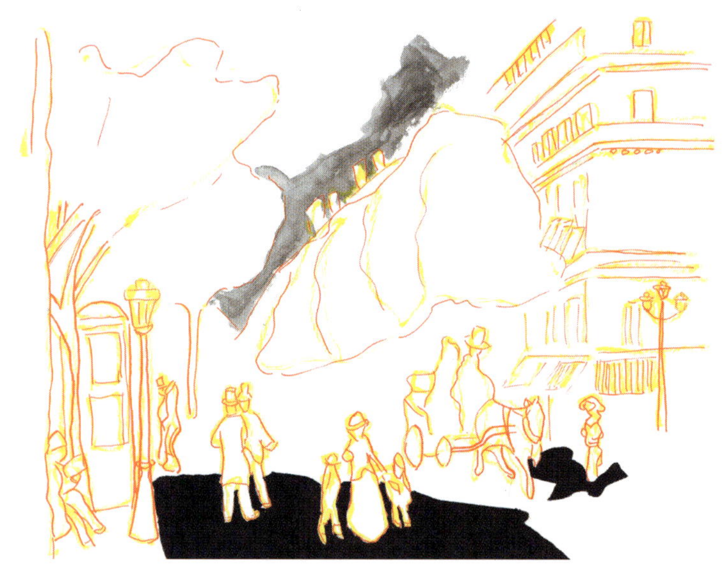

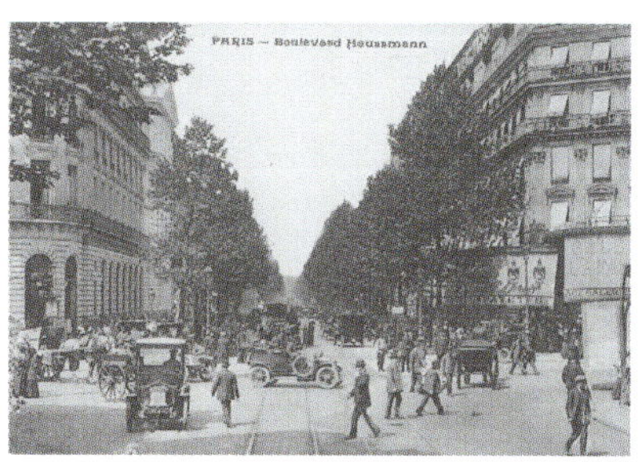

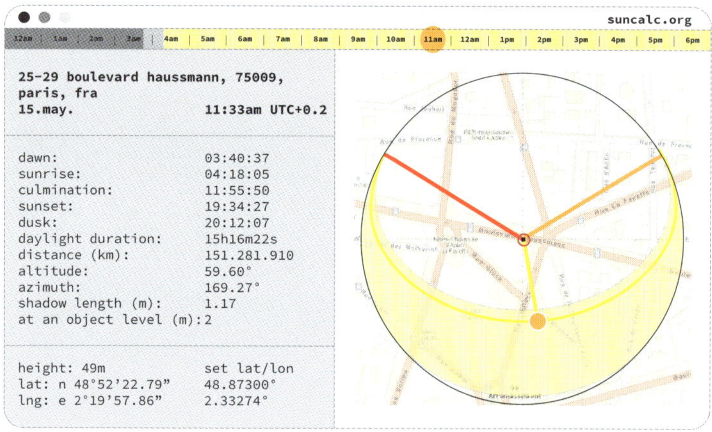

auguste renoir, *the grands boulevards*,
oil on canvas, 1875, 52.1 × 63.5 cm

the building on the right has two distinctive features: its two perpendicular sides are joined together by a corner façade at a 45° angle; balconies are running all along its third, fifth, and sixth floors. strolling along the boulevard haussmann and in *google street view*, building 38 seems to present the same features, at least in part, but its roof now boasts some kind of extension—today, it hosts the *galeries lafayette*. signs and construction work heavily modify the appearance the building had in 1875. in 1893, the great department store was only a 70 m² [753.47 sq. ft.] haberdashery shop: its story would really begin in 1912. a 1900 postcard shows what the building looked like at the time. its general character had already changed a bit because of large sun shades above the ground floor. but the sun shades had remained identical on the upper floors, and more importantly the plane trees had exactly

the same dimensions and appearance (they would disappear altogether a few years later). did renoir paint the *galeries lafayette before* the *galeries lafayette*?
it is springtime—the *flâneurs* are dressed in light clothes—the sun shines from the south, stretching to the north shadows that are about half the size of their original objects; it could be **11:33** a.m. it would be mid-may: according to *suncalc.org*, mid-may, a six-story building slightly less that 20 meters [65.62 ft.] high (3 meters [9.84 ft.] per story?) would cast a 12-meter [39.37 ft.] shadow. the boulevard haussmann is 30 meters [98.43 ft.] wide, the shadow from the building on the right is almost reaching the middle of the street; doing the math gives us similar length of shadows.
about the street furniture, three-armed street lights are set on concrete bases. in comparison to the

photograph taken in 1900, the lamp post in the painting is in a slightly different spot: would the construction of the *galeries lafayette* and the parisian metro have not only forced the street light to be moved to the right, but also to cut down the tree we discern on the right side of the painting? on the left, the simple lamp post already stands next to a *colonne morris* on the sidewalk. actually, to be exact, each of these things on the left side (the tree, the lamp post, and the *colonne morris*) occupy slightly different positions. twenty-five years have passed and, evidently, street furniture might have been moved. or maybe the painter played a little with the lines of perspective.

in a way, renoir is like an ancestor to the *google car*: he catches on the spot a view of pedestrians crossing the street, reading the newspaper, chatting. and like the *google car* does, he blurs their faces.

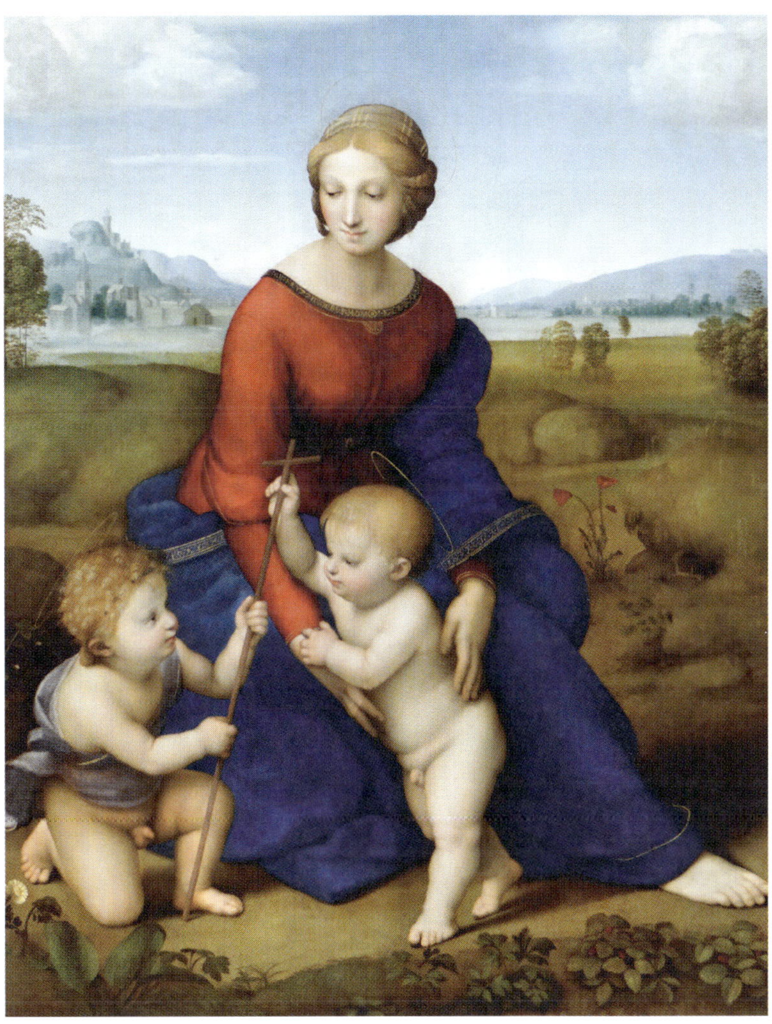

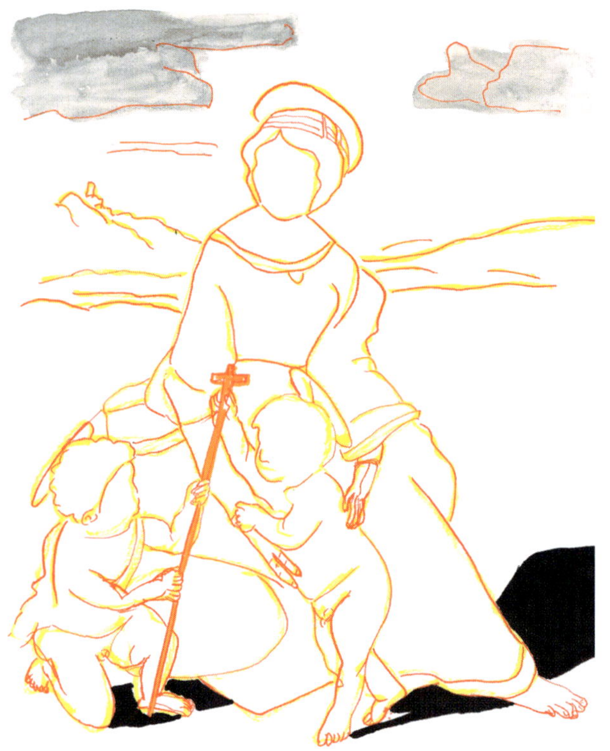

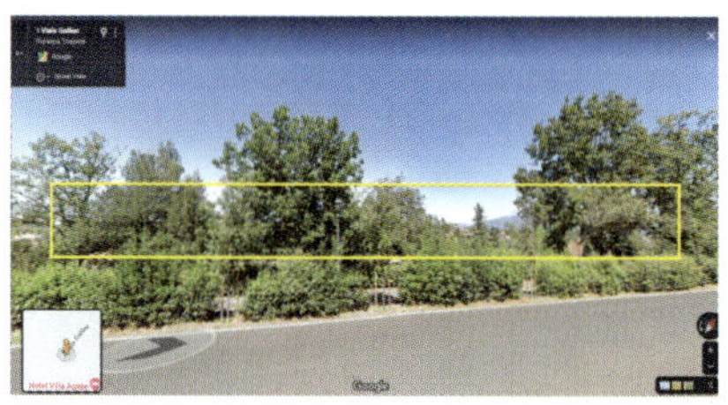

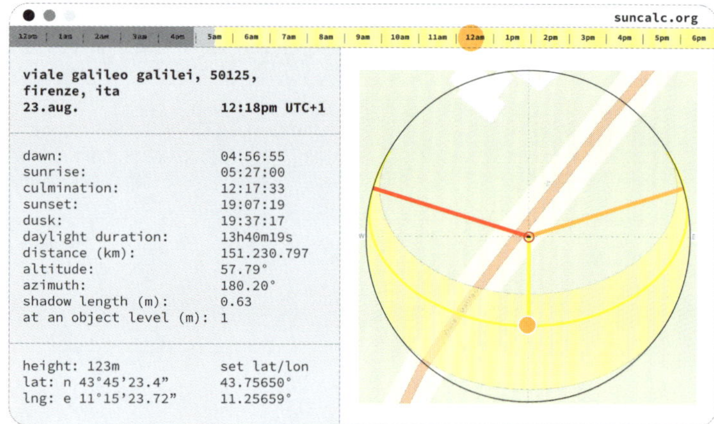

raphael (raffaello sanzio, known as), *madonna in the meadow*,
oil on canvas, 1505–1506, 113 × 88.5 cm

hard to pinpoint the location of this *madonna in the meadow*. the tuscan countryside stretches far and wide, but so do the many roads taken by the *google car*. offering visual access to hills with similar outlines, the *viale galileo* seems a good candidate—provided we accept the loss of the lake and its reflections of trees.

so, in this late summer of 1506 (the date is written on the hem of the dress), the air is soft, the children are playing innocently with a wooden cross. it's almost lunchtime, but who cares? it is **12:18** p.m.

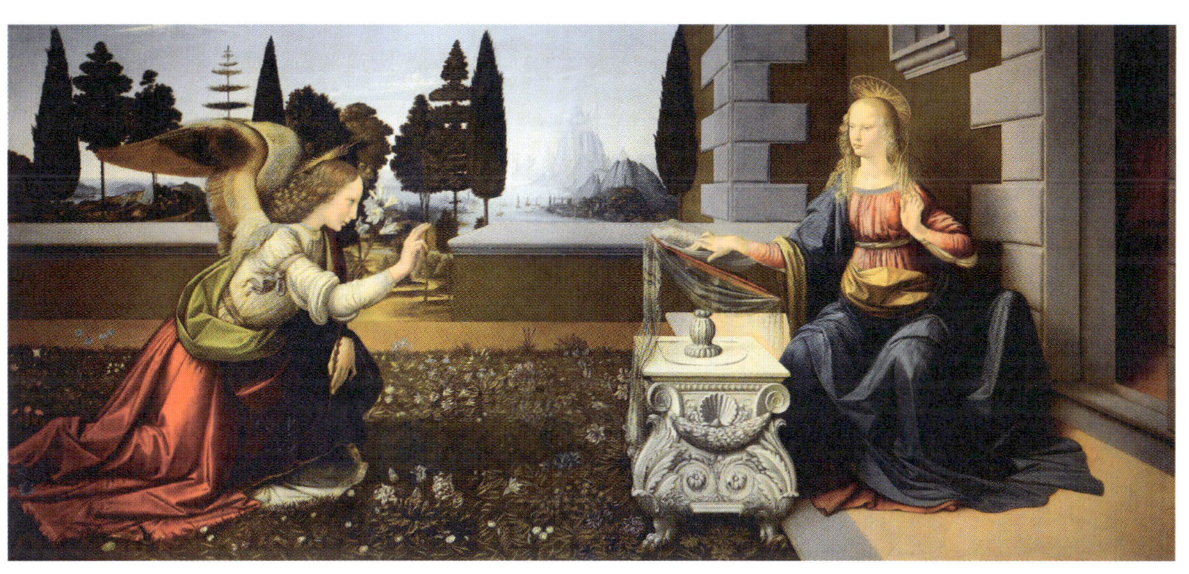

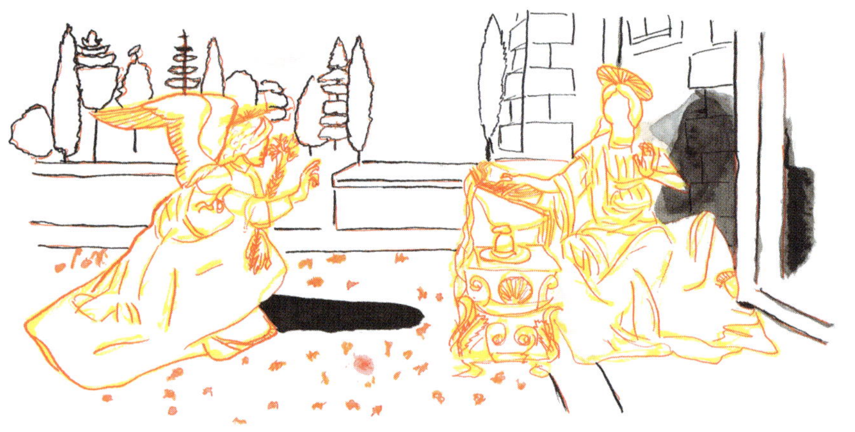

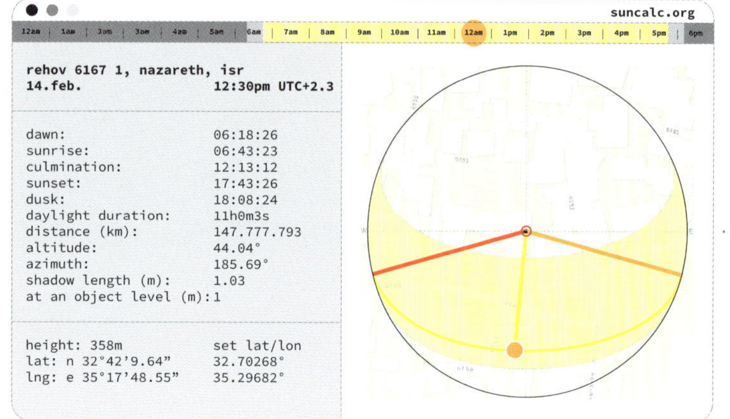

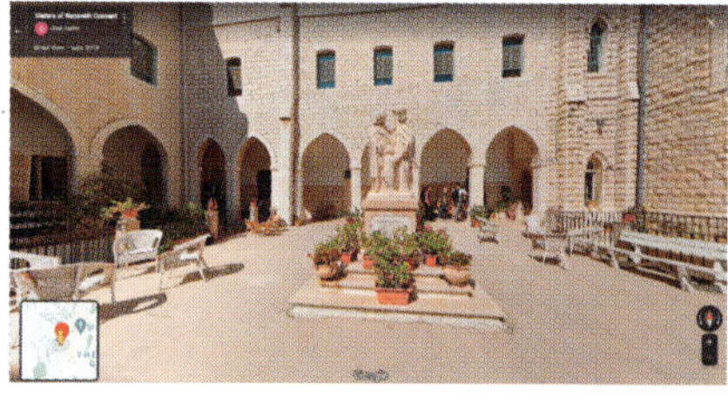

leonardo da vinci, ***annunciation***,
oil and tempera on wood panel, 1472, 98 × 217 cm

if, for many people, including *wikipedia*, the enclosed garden and its flowers symbolize nazareth—an erroneous etymology used to link “flower” and the town where mary was born—, then it must be conceded that the cave of the *annunciation* transformed into a little flower garden. nazareth is not a coastal town, so another concession would have to be that the boats featured in the background are navigating either the sea of galilee (24 km [14.91 mi.] away) or the mediterranean sea (haifa is only 30 km [18.64 mi.] away). by the way, according to daniel arasse, this is the first time a harbor is depicted in an annunciation. “what good can come from nazareth?,” someone said in *the gospel of john*, already lamenting about this village.
pines and cypresses are pruned the florentine way; topiary art cuts trees into clouds, round wheels, or tiered obelisks. is it because nazareth and florence are twinned cities nowadays?

it is also purported that mary was reading the bible when the archangel gabriel interrupted. yet it is impossible to discern what book lies under the veil on the lectern—but what would mary read other than the bible? (the old testament, obviously, the new one still had to be written—unless there existed an antecryphal version, or maybe it had been released as a "working paper"). it is impossible as well to know which page or what passage she is reading.

in nazareth, archeologists found no trace whatsoever of synagogues dating back to the period of jesus' lifetime. the famous cave was turned into a basilica (that was destroyed by an earthquake in 1102). mary's house has become a convent for nazareth's nuns. if we're in the courtyard of today's convent, then mary is sitting north, and gabriel, south. with the sun behind his back, the kneeling angel casts a shadow almost his own size indicating it is **12:30** p.m. the equivalence between length and height takes us to a fairly premature february 14: since the birth was planned for december 25, its cause should have occurred around march 25—or even april 6, if we consider january 6 as the original birth date of jesus. march 25 was already quite a busy day: besides the spring equinox, christian tradition holds that it is the first day of *genesis*, the day of the fall of adam and eve, the day of the sacrifice of isaac, the day of the death of jesus on the cross, the day of judgment day, and more. the exact time hasn't been disclosed.

for a while, february 14 was the date of the *hypapante* (a *pidyon haben*, or redemption of the first born, using a pseudonym), but it automatically moved backwards to february 2 after january 6 was advanced in history to december 25.

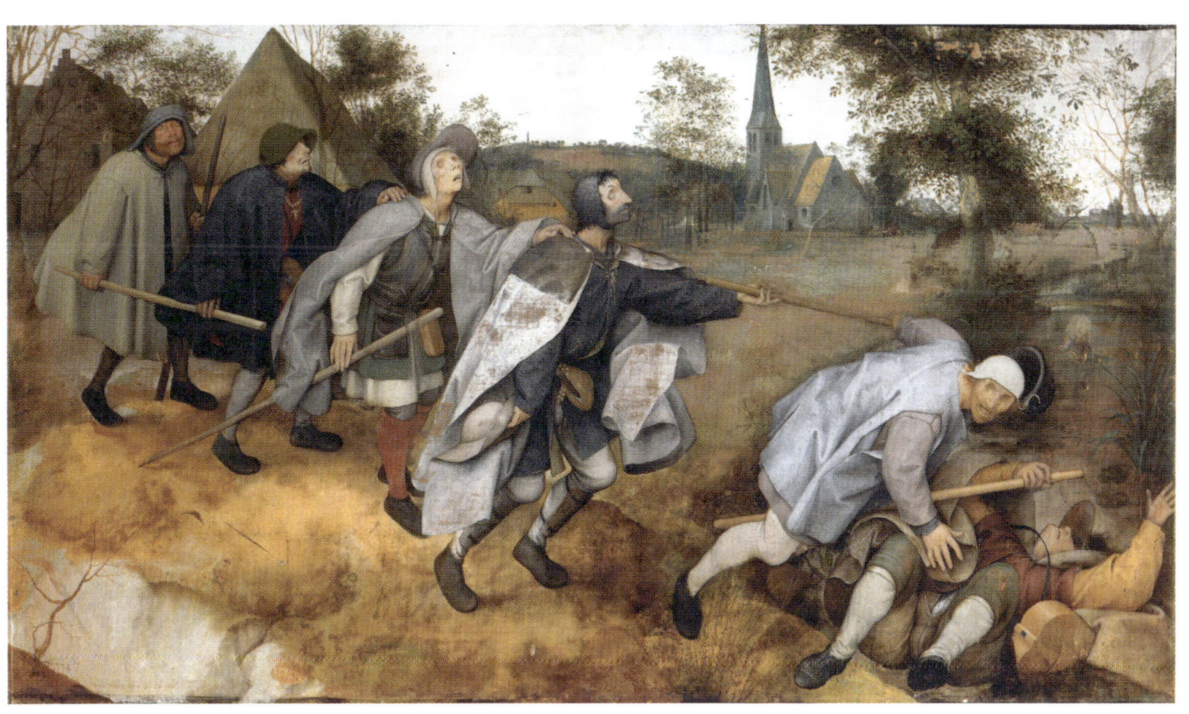

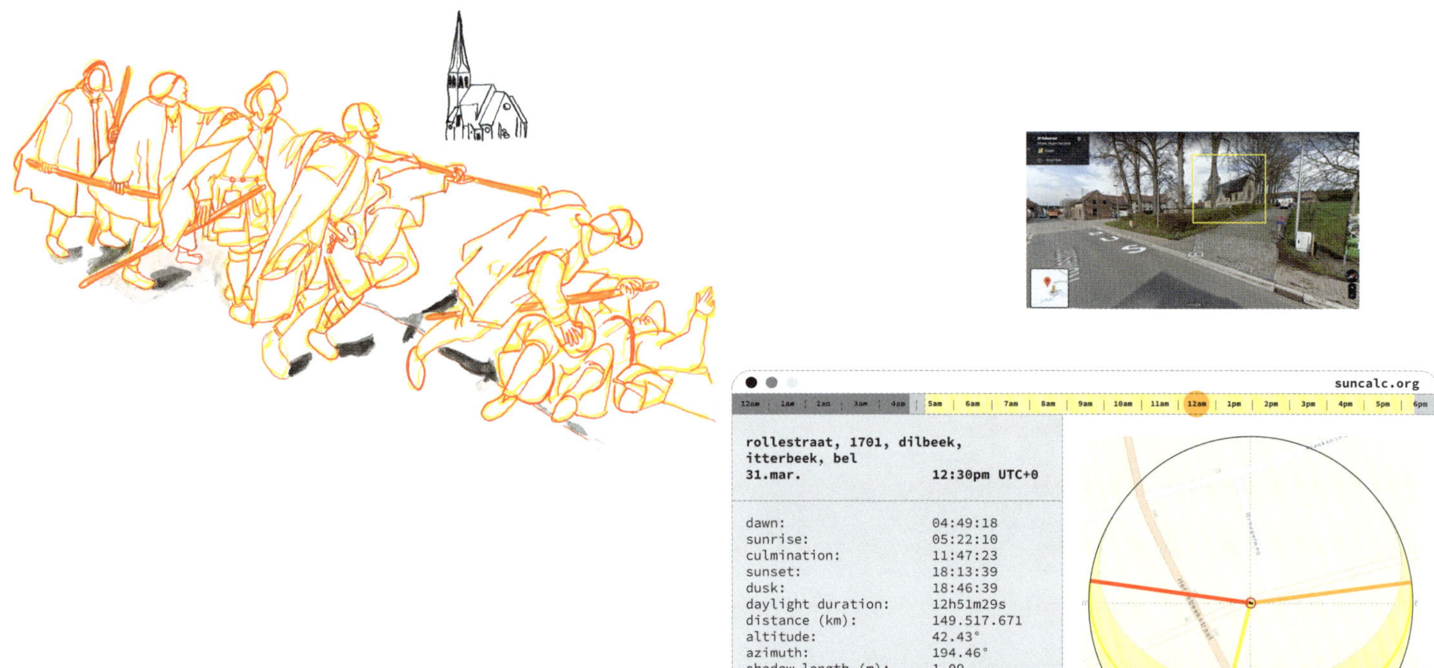

pieter brueghel the elder, ***the parable of the blind***,
tüchlein on canvas, 1568, 86 × 154 cm

oh, sure, the sky is gray on that very day of march 31, as the clock strikes **12:30** p.m. but did they really see it?
in the background, the sint-anna church of sint-anna-pede.

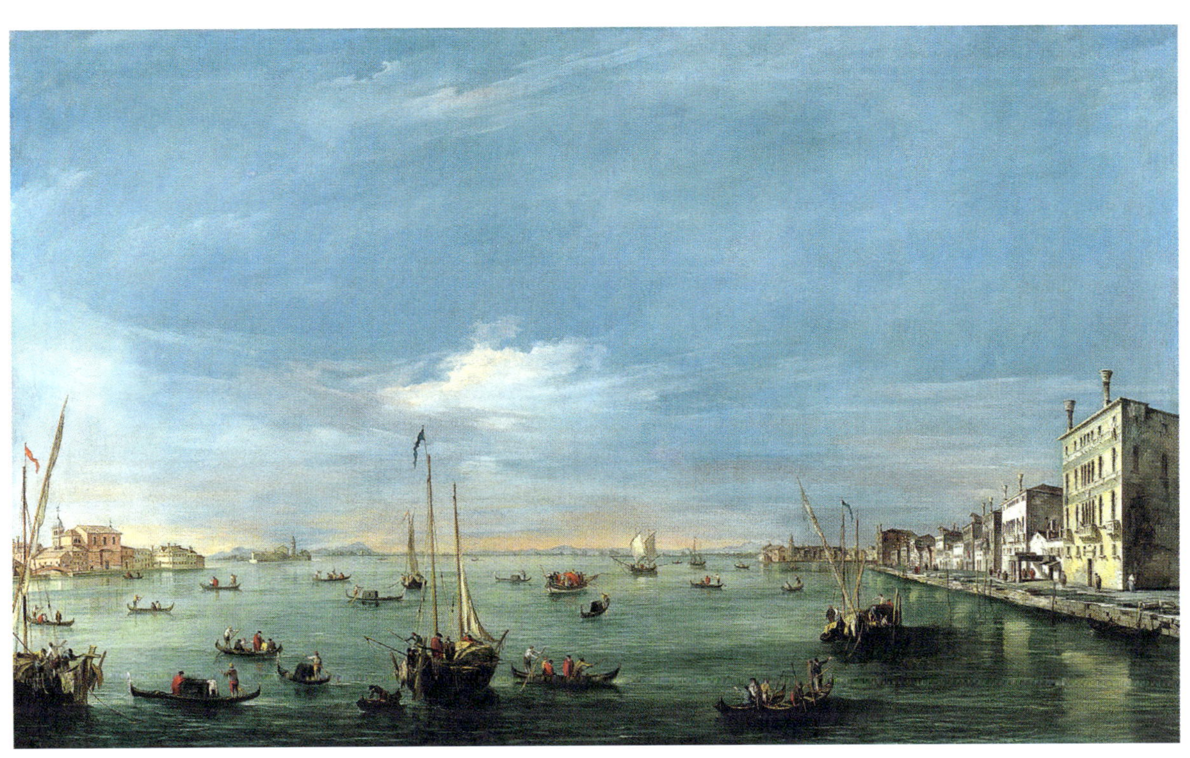

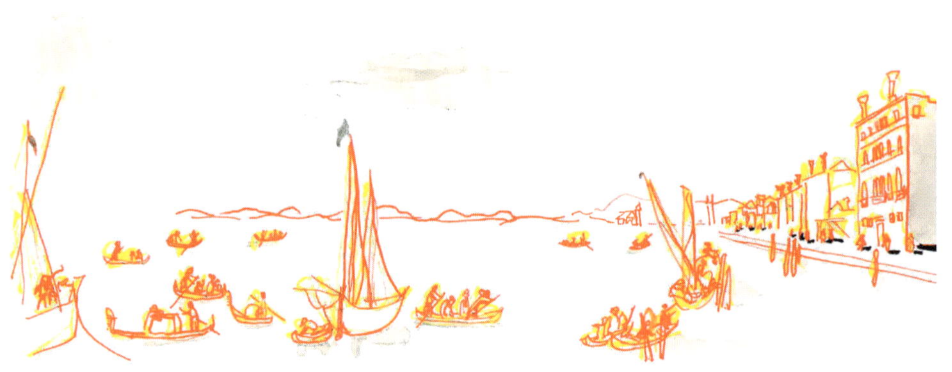

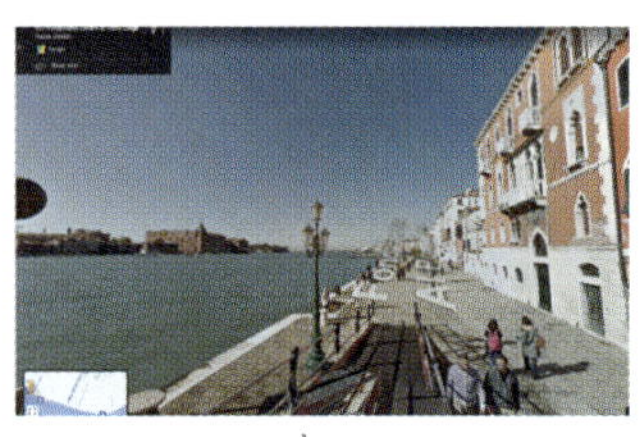

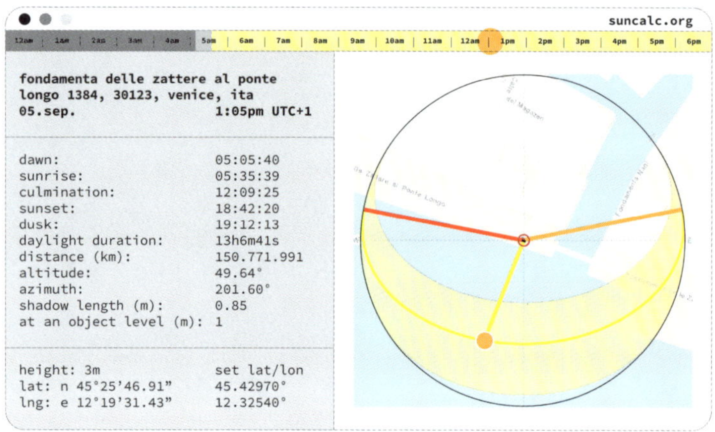

francesco guardi, *view of the giudecca canal and the zattere*, oil on canvas, 1757–1758, 72.2 × 119.3 cm

contrary to what some art historians believe, the sun never sets in this painting by guardi. the reflections of the boats in the water are not helpful at all: the position of the sun and its orientation do not affect them in any way. luckily, there's always land to rely upon. the shadows some characters cast on the *zattere* promenade are perpendicular to the ground, slightly shorter than the height of the people. the time is **1:05** p.m., either in early april or early september.

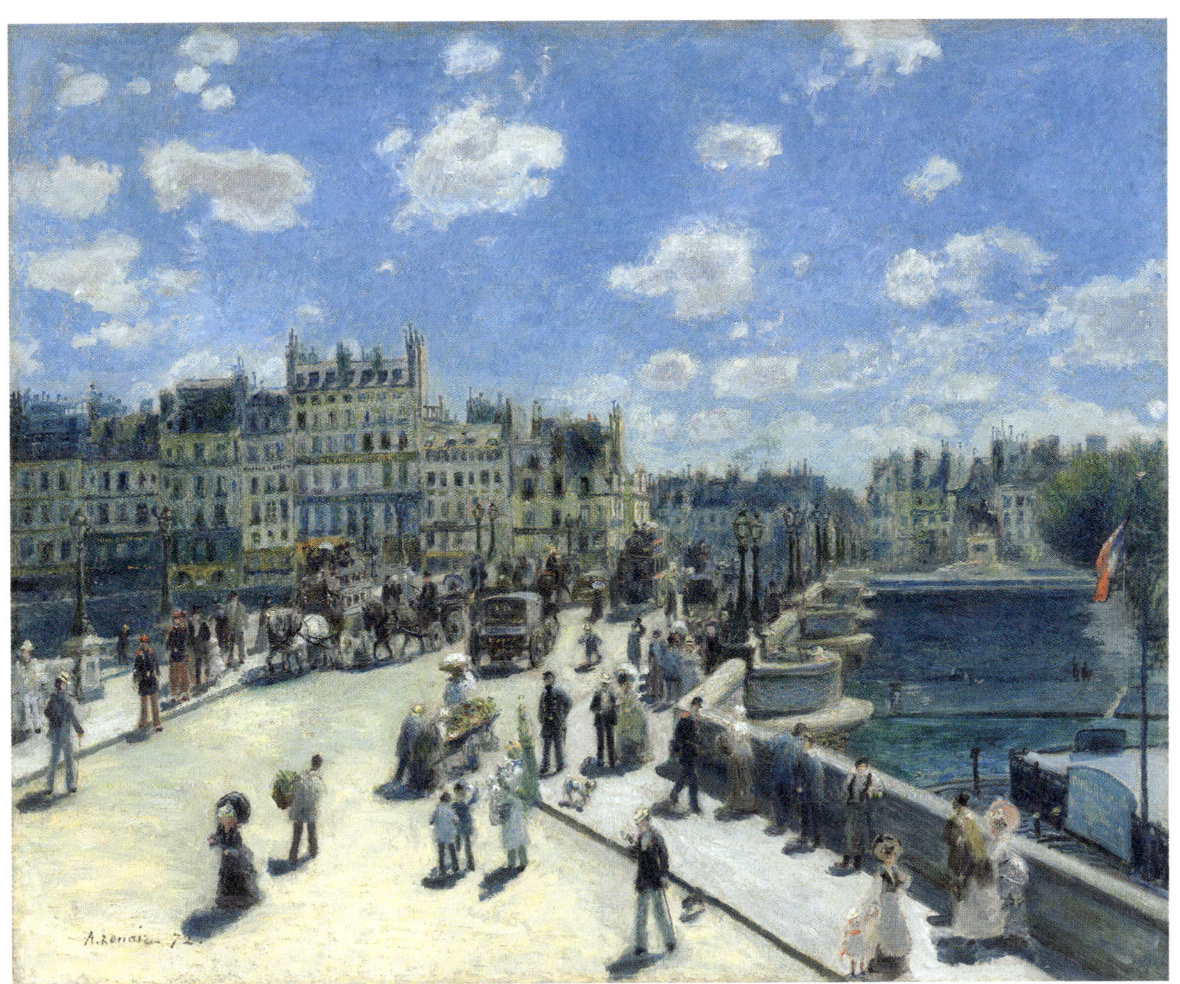
A. Renoir. 72.

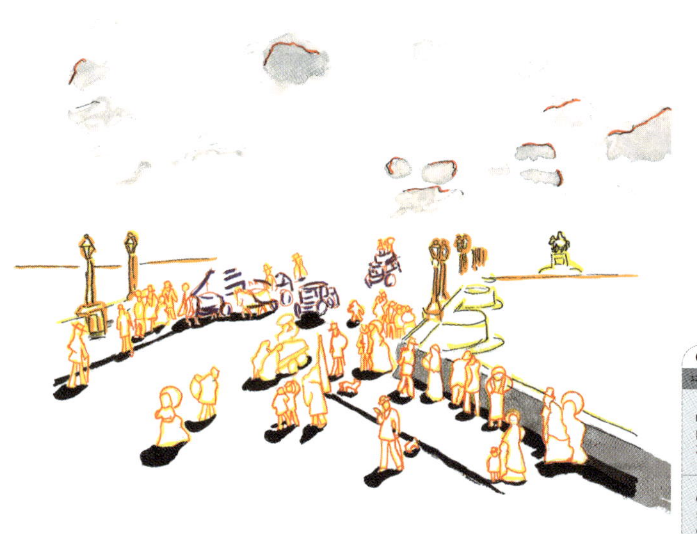

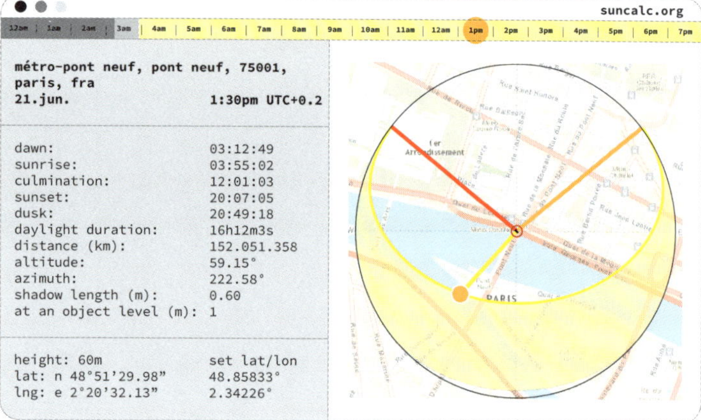

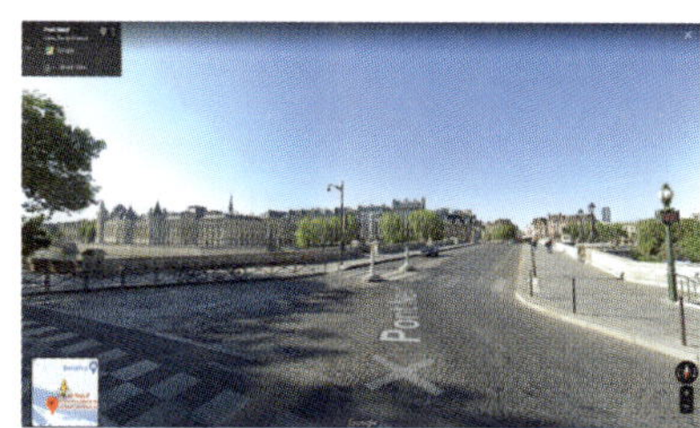

auguste renoir, ***pont neuf, paris***,
oil on canvas, 1872, 74 × 92 cm

it's june, it's the *pont neuf*, it's paris. at the end of the bridge, the south.
the shadows of the people walking around are shorter than they are. it's probably early afternoon, after lunch, around **1:30** p.m. the sun is so high in the sky that it is outside the frame.

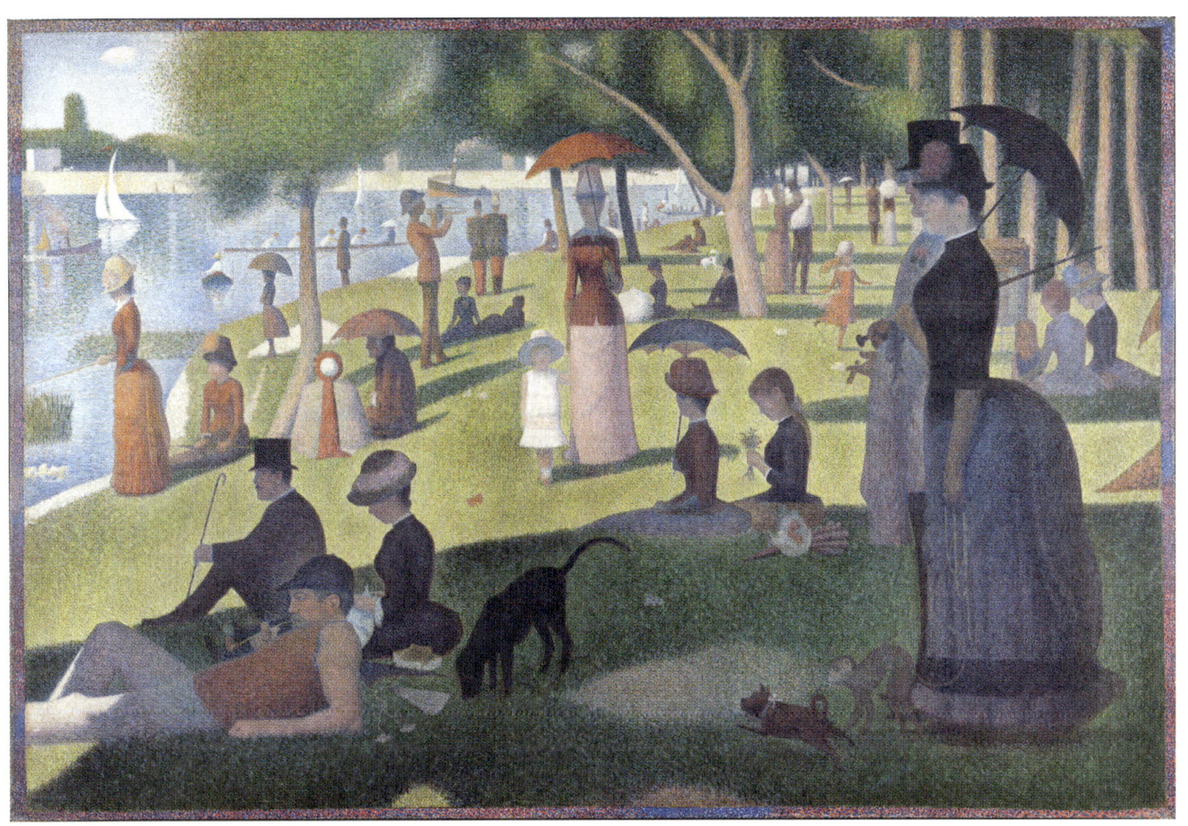

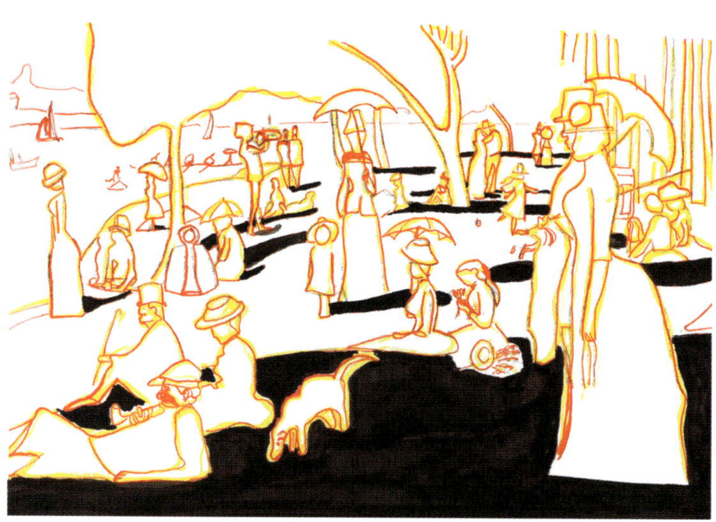

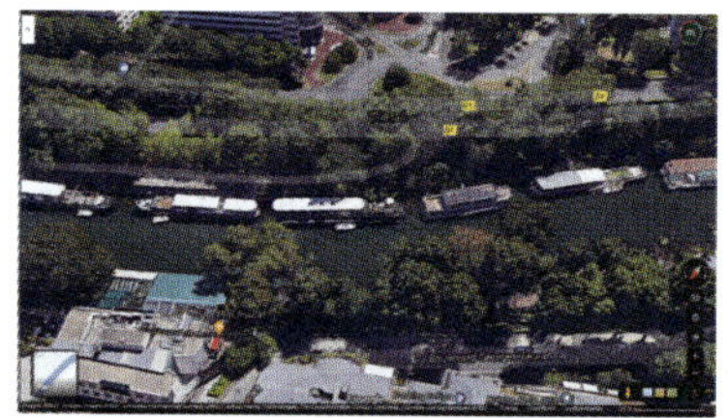

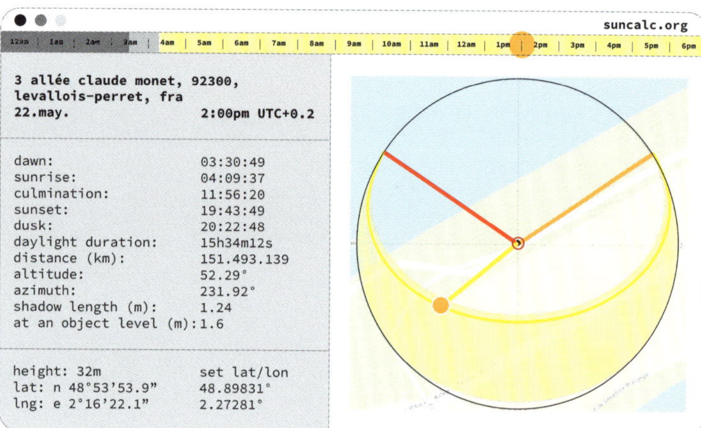

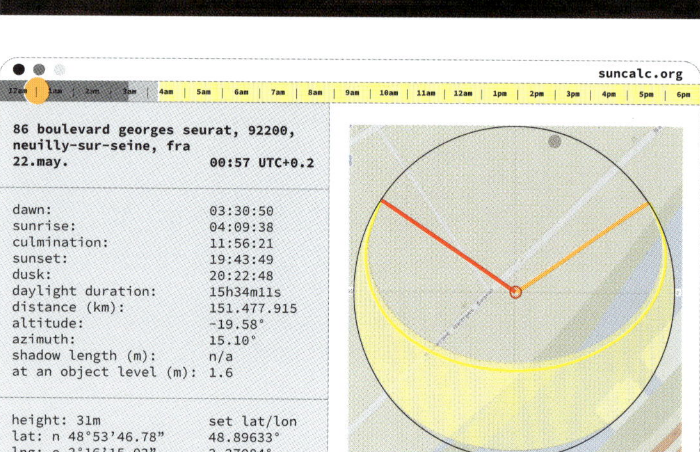

georges seurat, study for *a sunday afternoon on la grande jatte*, oil on canvas, 1884, 70.5 × 104.1 cm

seurat states that he started the studies for *a sunday afternoon on the island of la grande jatte* and the painting itself on thursday, may 22, 1884, which was ascension day. *la grande jatte* island is located near neuilly, between two arms of the river seine, and does have two shores, one facing southeast, the other northeast. in the case of the former, next to boulevard georges seurat, *suncalc.org* tells us the shadows depicted in the painting could never occur in real life (the time would be **12:57** a.m.). the latter riverbank, claude monet alley, sounds like a more reasonable option: **2:00** p.m. it's a good time to take a nap, but no one seems to be dozing off. no trace of any luncheon on the grass either. must fifty years pass for such unspeakable activities to take hold, thanks to the introduction of paid vacations?

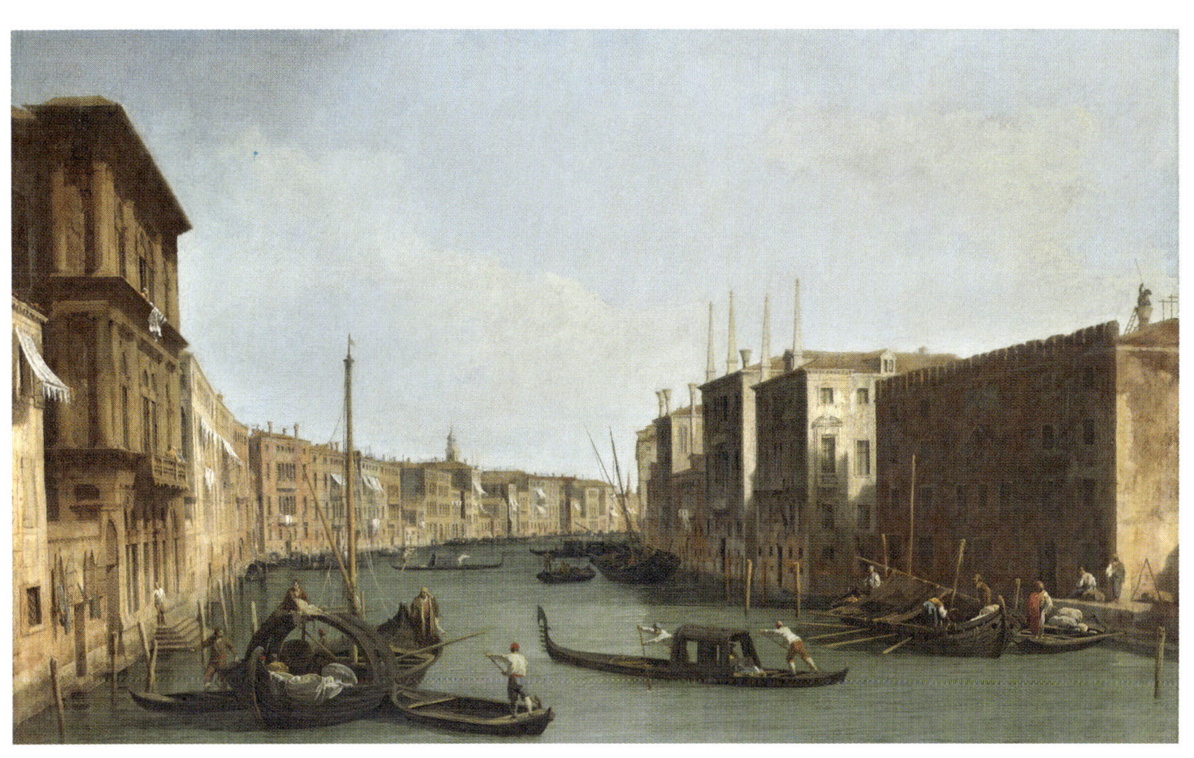

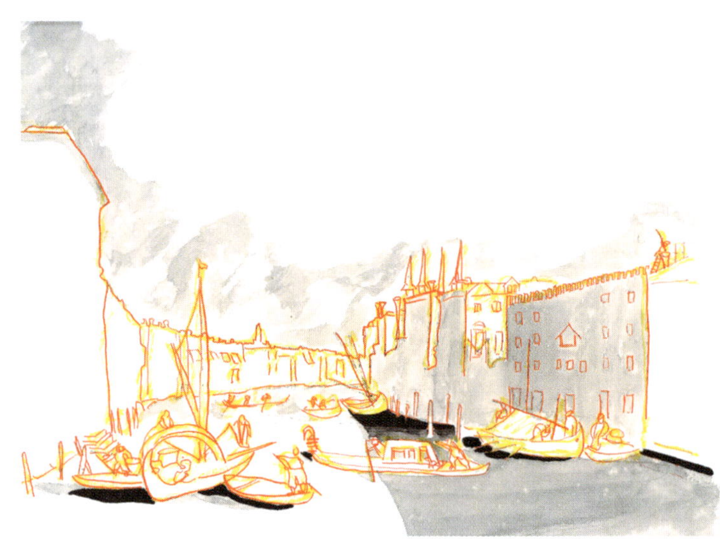

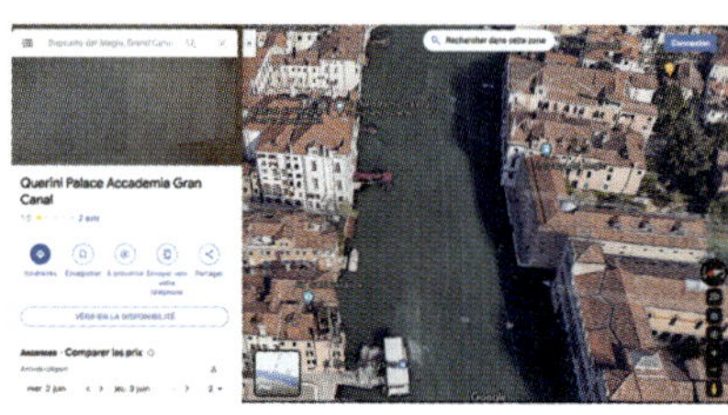

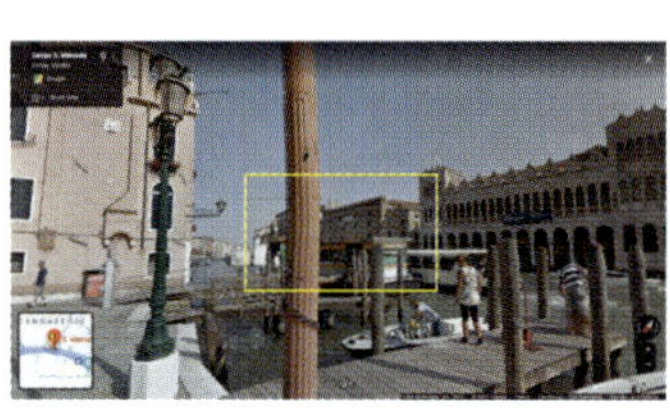

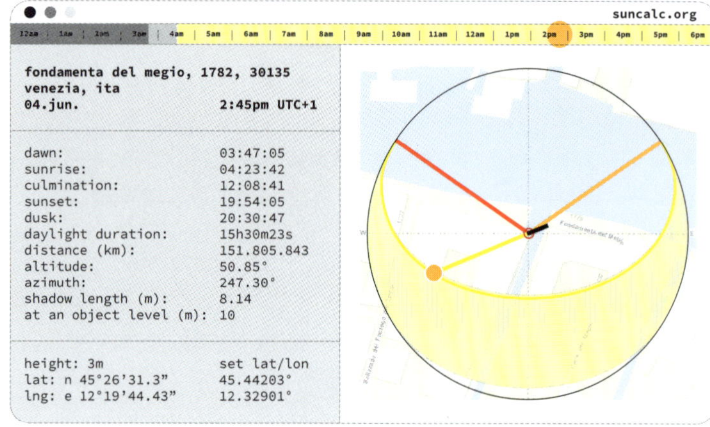

canaletto (giovanni antonio canal, known as), *view of the grand canal*,
oil on canvas, c. 1728–1729, 60.3 × 100.3 cm

the first building on the right is easily recognizable, it's the *deposito del megio*. on the left, the large protruding building is the *palazzo vendramin calergi*. the shadows are difficult to make out, for they differ from the reflections in the water. if the *deposito del megio* does cast the shadow of its right corner on the side of the neighboring building, then the sun would be southwest, on the right side of the painting (the shadows of a few gondoliers seem to stretch in the same direction). on the right bank, the facades do not receive direct light. since the buildings are bigger than their shadows, maybe it is early june. the time would be **2:45** p.m. the weather is mild, the men have rolled up their shirt sleeves.

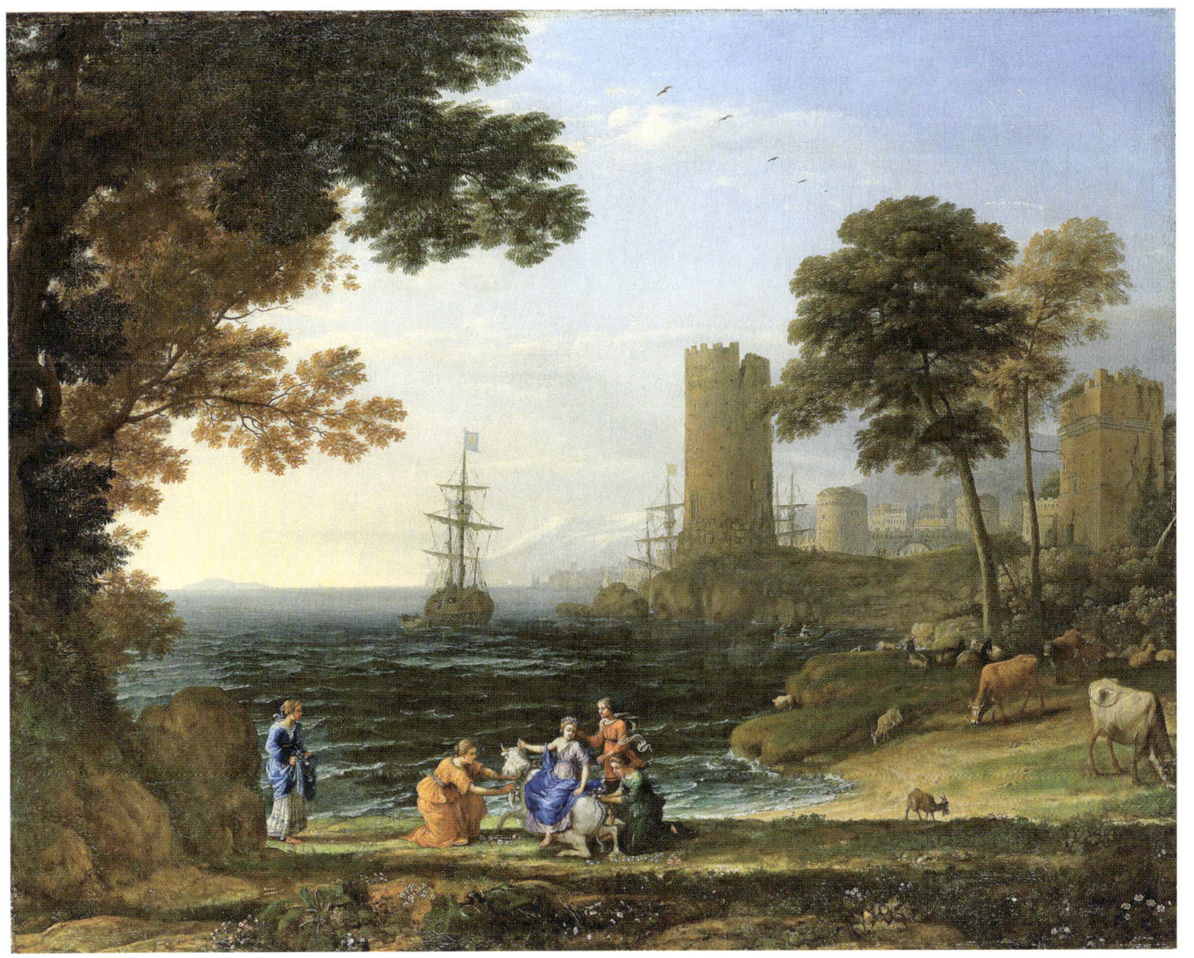

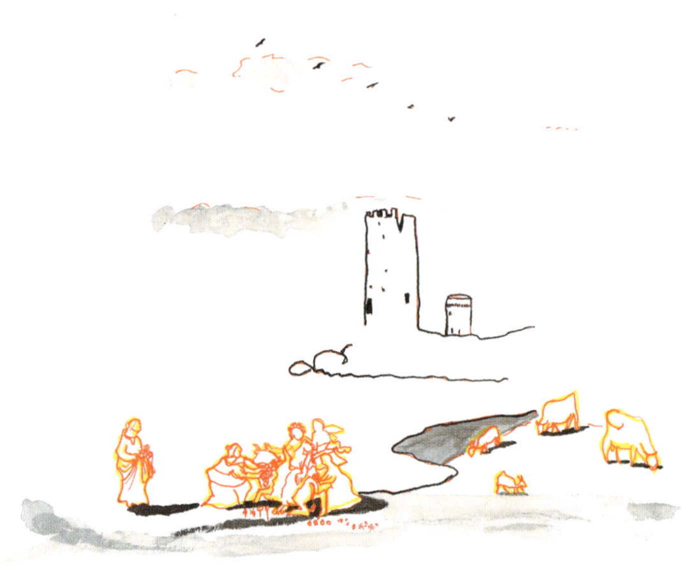

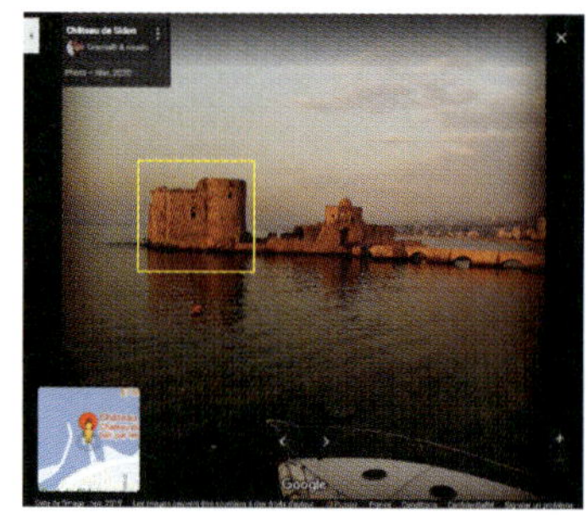

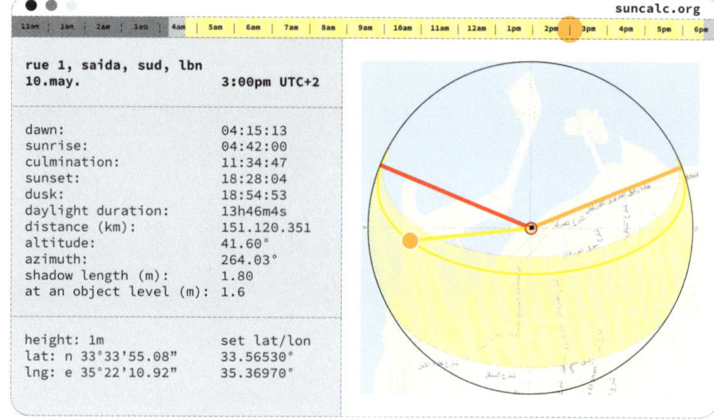

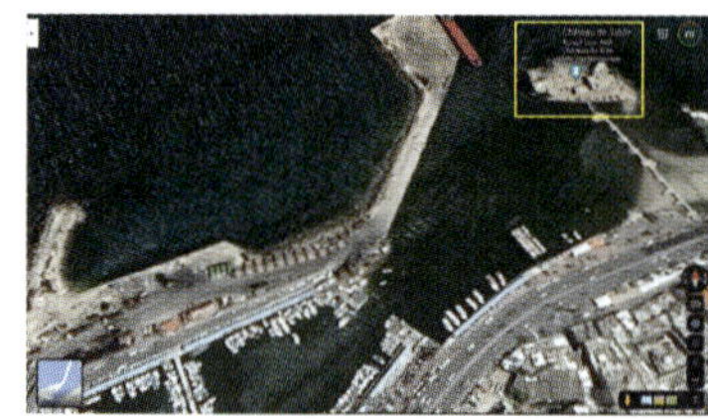

le lorrain (claude gellée, known as), *the rape of europa*, oil on canvas, 1645 ?, 96.2 × 167.6 cm

even though claude gellée has often painted towers that stand near the entrance of seaports (*landscape with aeneas at delos, seaport with the embarkation of the queen of sheba, morning at the port*—which used to be called *in the evening* until 1955), we know that europa was kidnapped near sidon (today also known as sayda) in lebanon by zeus—who had taken the form of a white bull so as not to raise suspicions. the shadow is slightly more elongated than the vertical object casting it.
contrary to those who think that light coming from the left denotes a cold morning, it is **3:00** p.m. in early may.

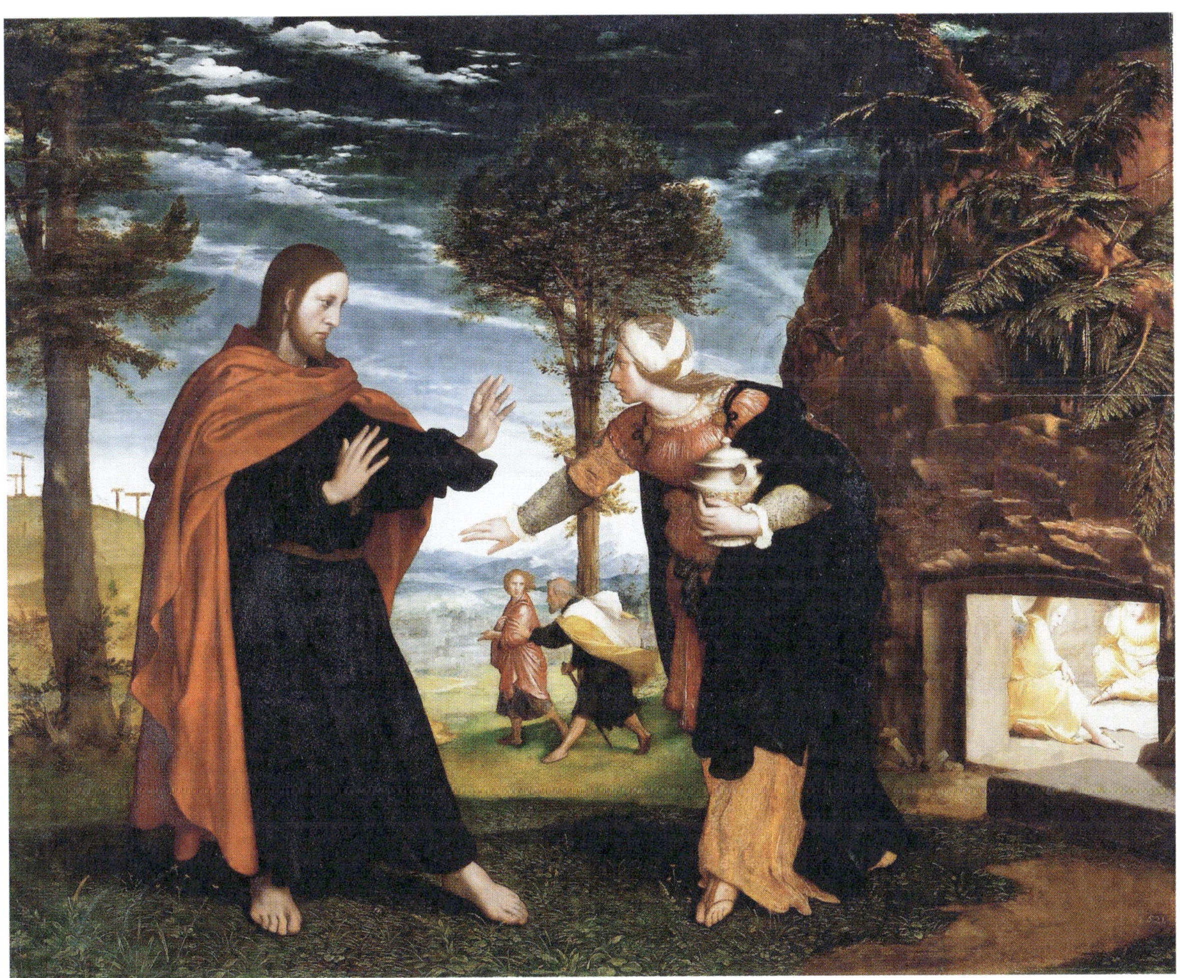

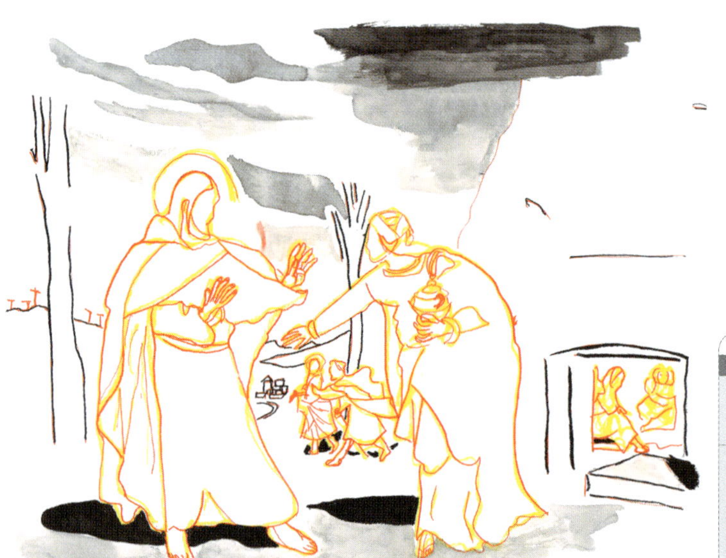

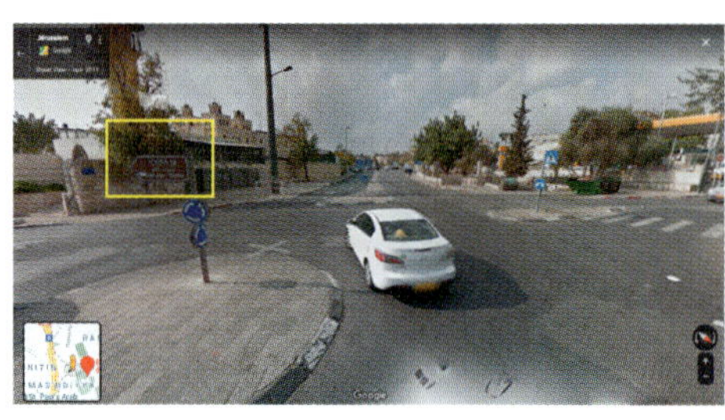

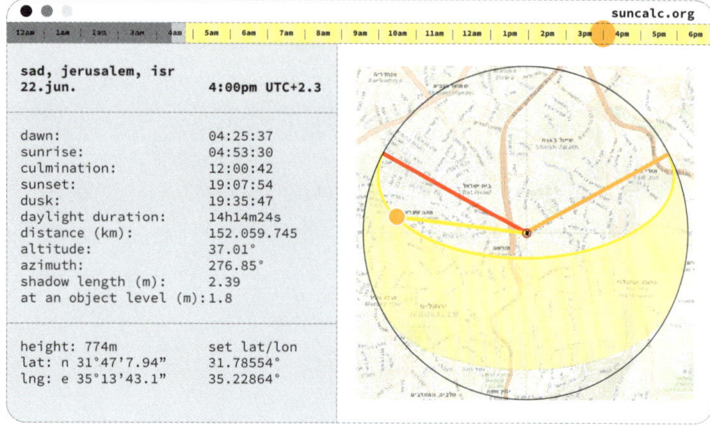

hans holbein the younger, *noli me tangere*,
oil on canvas, 1526–1528, 76.7 × 95.8 cm

north of golgotha, or in the english countryside, circa 1526–1528?
mary magdalene goes to jesus' tomb. she finds two angels in lieu of the corpse—here it's a cave that stands for the vault. turning around, she sees jesus standing up and calling her by name. she recognizes him: "rabbi!" he warns her: "don't touch me!"
the gospels say that mary magdalene goes to the vault in the first hours immediately following shabbat, before sunrise. a very early sunday morning, then. passover generally takes place in april.
if jerusalem is in the background and golgotha is on the left with its *tau*-shaped crosses, the scene would be happening north-northwest of the city, on a hill more or less as tall as that of golgotha. probably beyond the damascus gate, towards *derekh shrem*, on the road to *sheikh jarrah*. "gordon's calvary" a.k.a. the "garden tomb" is also a plausible site. the place where the crucifixion happened and the tomb are therefore geographically apart: holbein refutes helena, constantine's mother, who believed the tomb to be situated where the church of the holy sepulcher stands today, within the walls of jerusalem.
the sky might be dark, but it is clearing up in the south. however, the characters in the background are casting their shadows from the west. for *suncalc.org*, their moderate length would lead us to the beginning of summer, at the end of june, around **4:00** p.m., rather than dawn in april (then, the length of the shadows would be a match in the middle of the morning, though the sun would travel from east to south, facing us).
yet, in the foreground, the true source of light comes from the cave, full of the presence of the angels. the time of the painting is indeed that of the angels.

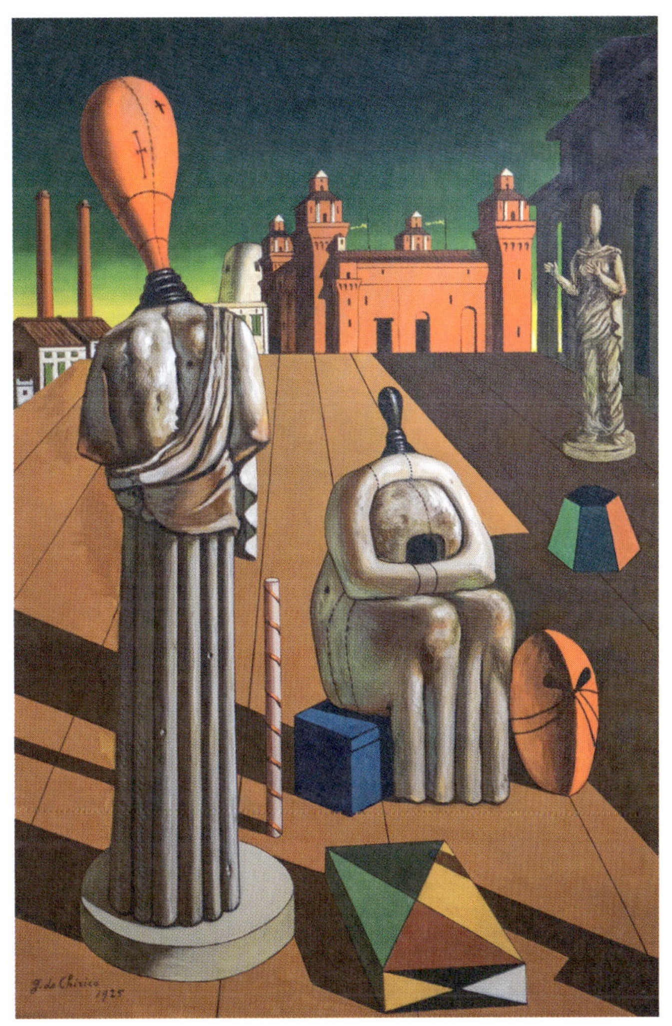
G. de Chirico
1925

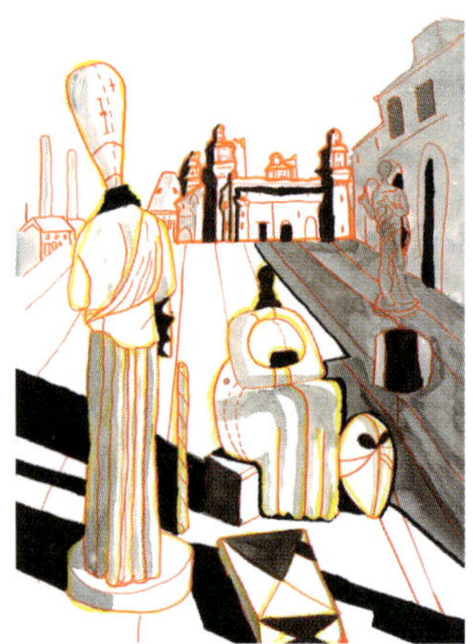

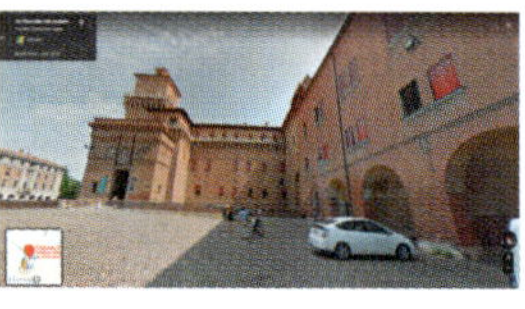

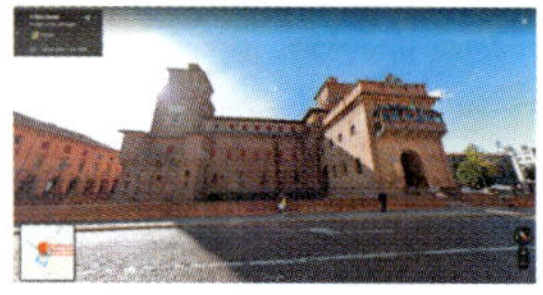

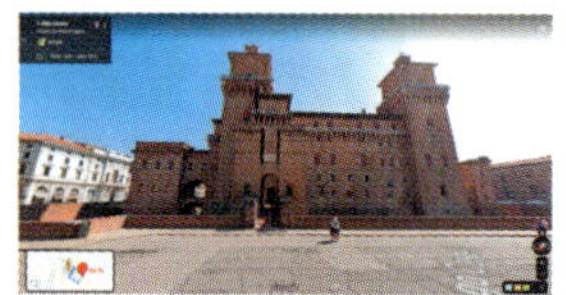

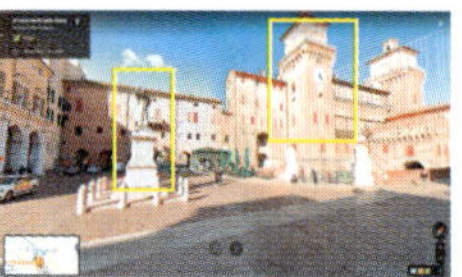

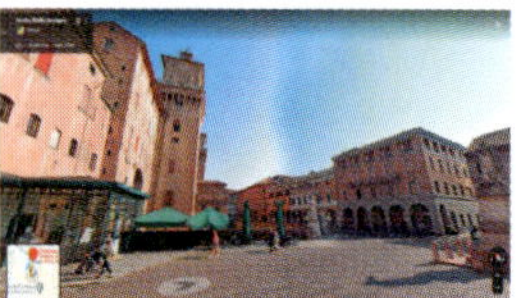

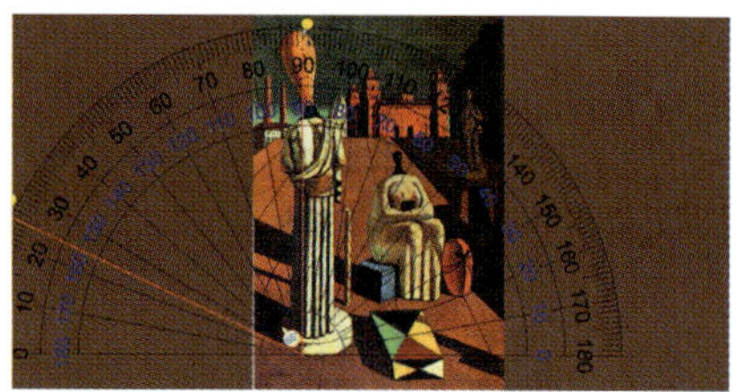

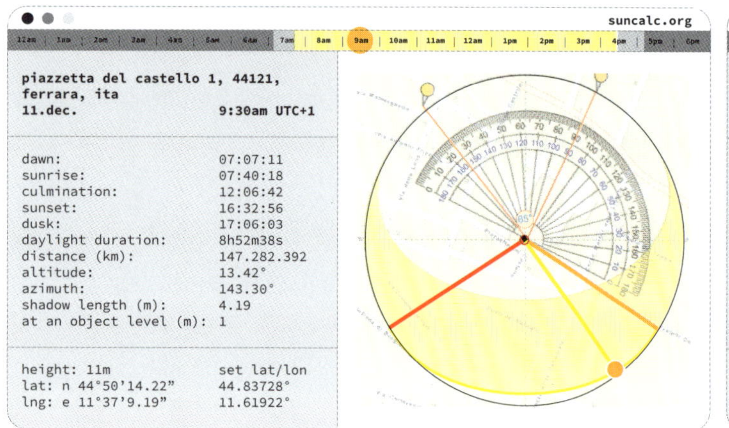

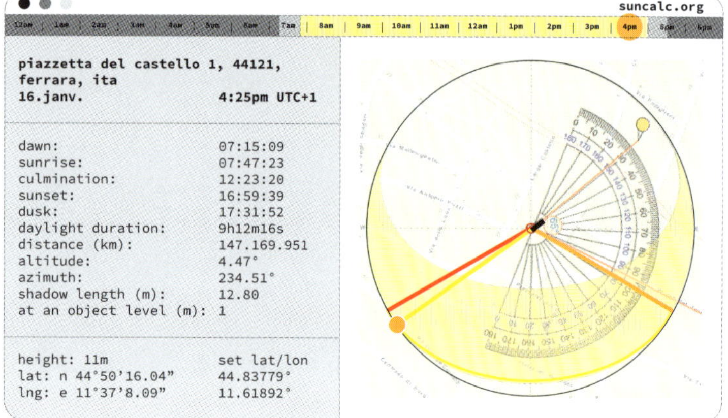

giorgio de chirico, *the disquieting muses*,
oil on canvas, 1917–1918, 97 × 67 cm

the *google street view* car goes all the way around the glorious castello estense in ferrara, but it's no use: none of its sides match the painting. one comes fairly close, but its clock has vanished from the canvas. another detail is puzzling: the statue on its left side would be reversed in comparison to that in the painting, whose arm hangs low. would the position of the shadows on the ground come to the rescue, once again? (what is this strange object outside the frame, only revealed by its shadow?)

the shadow of the woman sitting down seems to be more than twice or thrice as long as the object casting it—what's more, it continues past the frame of the painting, and where it ends remains unknown to us. how embarrassing.

suncalc allows us to make a decision: for a shadow to form a 65° angle or so with the facade, only two sides of the building are staying in the running: the south side—it would be a little past **9:30** a.m. in december, 1917, and a 1-meter [3.28 ft.] high object would cast a 4-meter [13.12 ft.] long shadow; and the west side, in mid-january of the same year, around **4:25** p.m., a 1-meter [3.28 ft.] high object casting a 12-meter [39.37 ft.] long shadow at least. the twilight sky would tip the scales in favor of the latter.

is metaphysical painting actually out of any and all seasons?

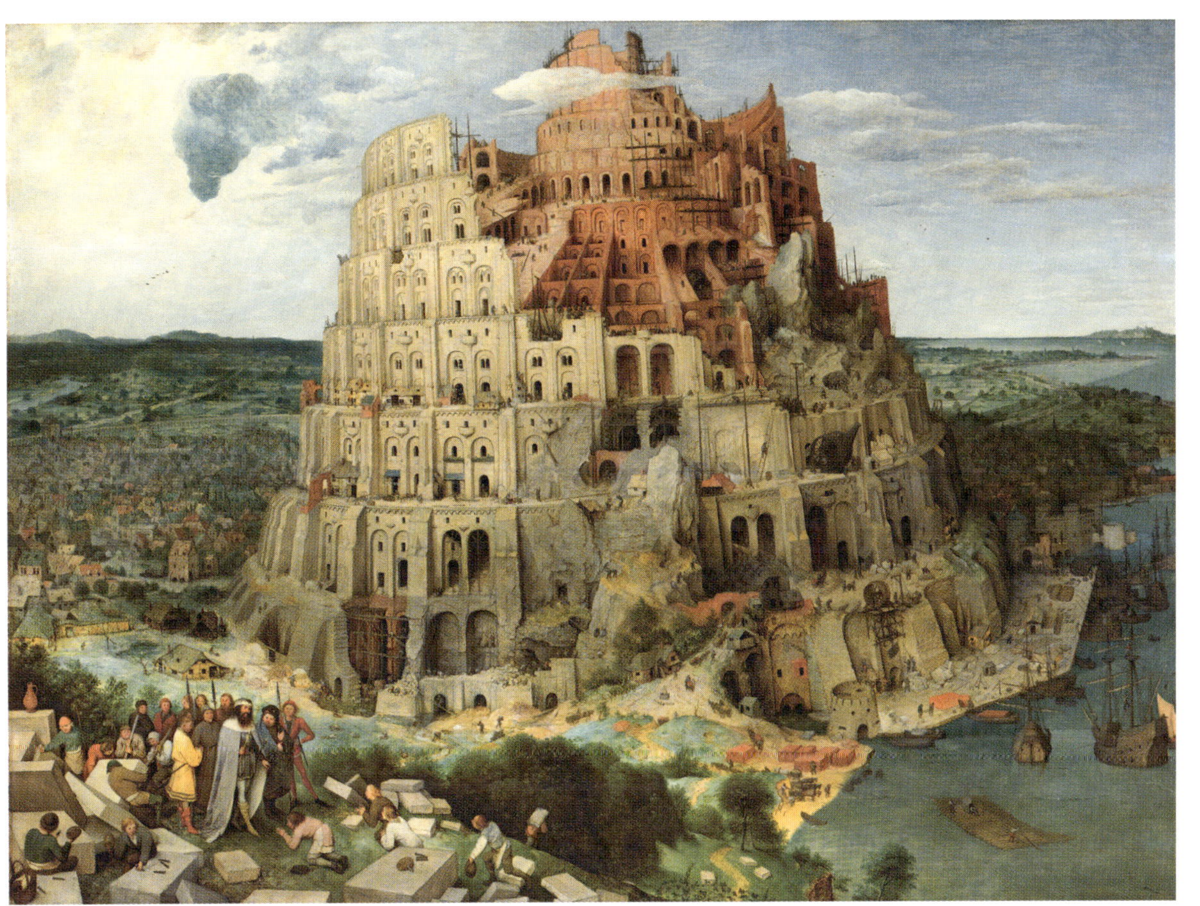

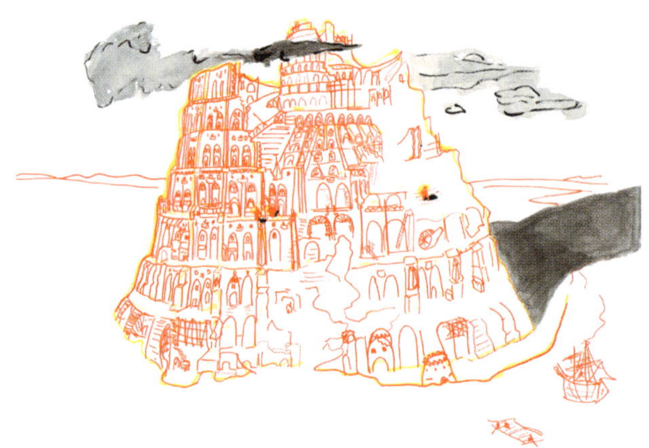

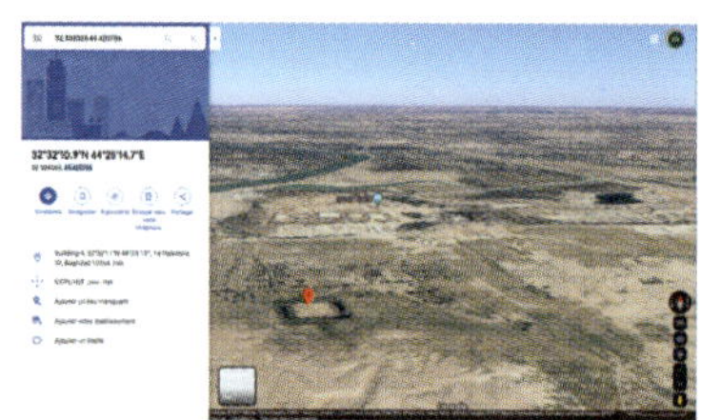

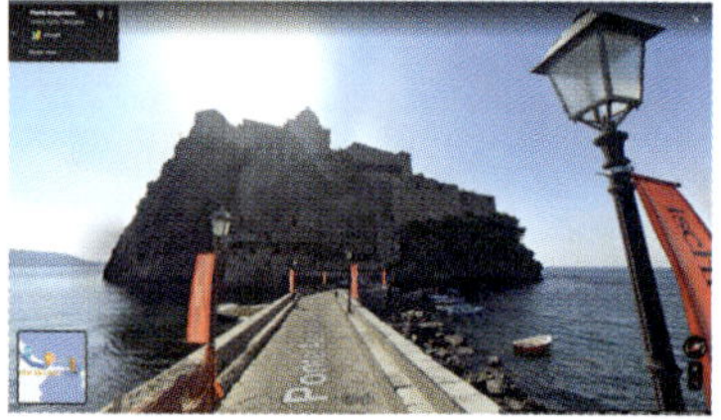

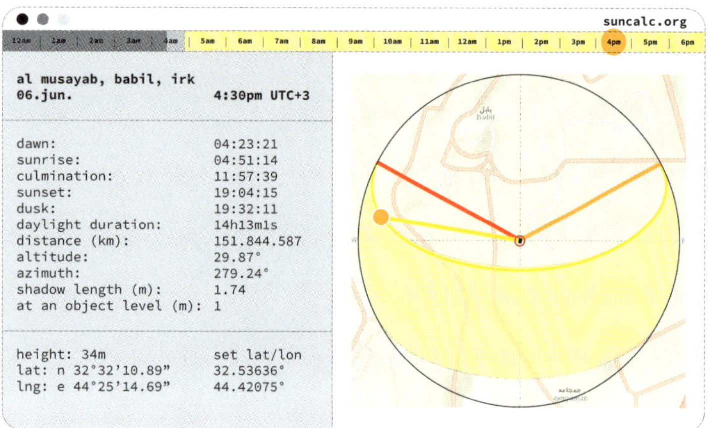

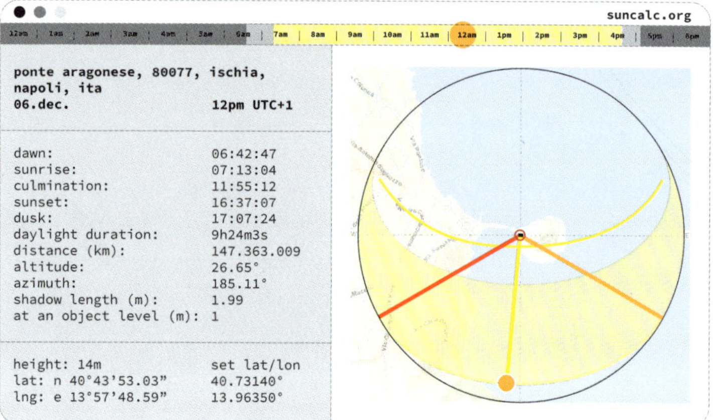

pieter brueghel the elder, *the tower of babel*,
oil on convas, 1563, 114 × 155 cm

there are workers, construction sites, materials being transported. some cook, others hang out their laundry—the tower hosts the many tasks of daily life. favelas are already there, and some makeshift shelters, made of canvas or cob, stand as buttresses to the stone facades—a city within the city, a tower within the tower; the insignificant proletarian builders live there, surviving as best they can. the sky is opening up on the left, and the tower itself casts its gigantic shadow on the right side of the city, but there are nevertheless not that many shadows in this painting. here and there, we can guess some worker's shadow. but still, from one floor to another, from one section to another, their orientation differ. has anyone ever registered the different time zones of the tower of babel?

according to *wikipedia*, there are two towers of babel. the first is in babylonia—in iraq today. *google street view* locates it fairly easily. but as it was destroyed such a long time ago, it's impossible to know how it was oriented. the length of the shadows nevertheless suggests it's early june, maybe around **4:30** p.m.

back in the day, the area was fertile. alright. but so fertile that an actual lake would allow the many boats to line up alongside the tower?

the other tower can be found on the island of ischia, connected to the coast of campania. there, a castle stands, which might have inspired the painter. everything is suddenly upended: the shadow means december, the clock has just struck **12:00** p.m.

what justifies such a big difference? the one-hour gap between the two timezones cannot explain such a discrepancy.

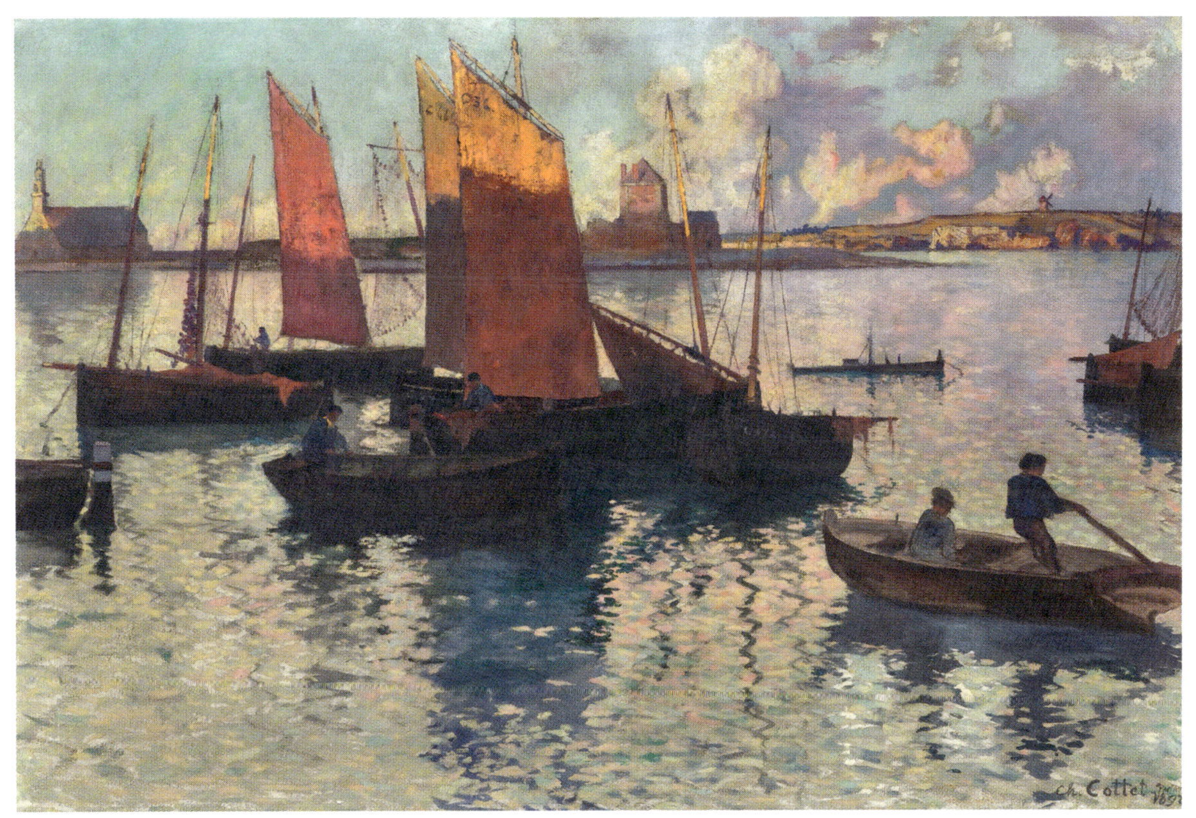
Ch. Cottet

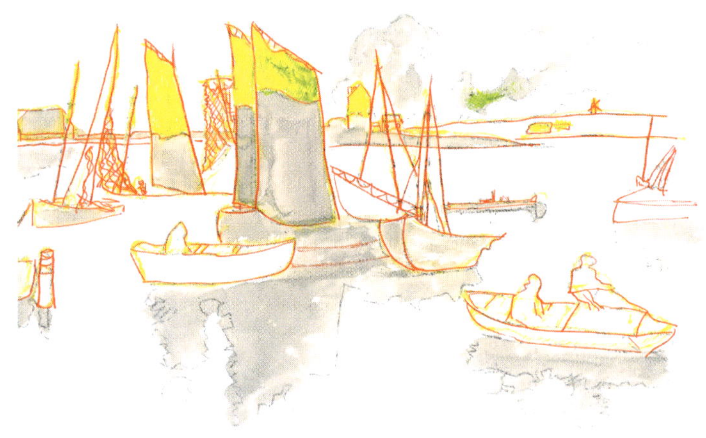

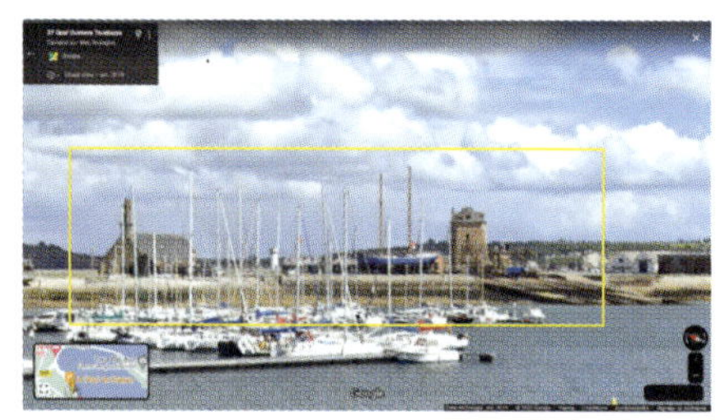

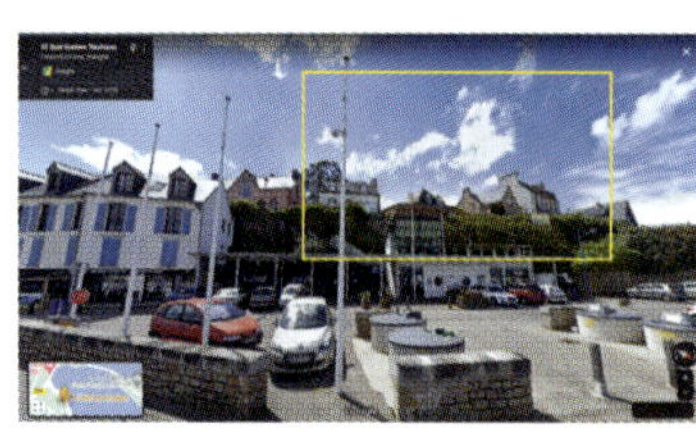

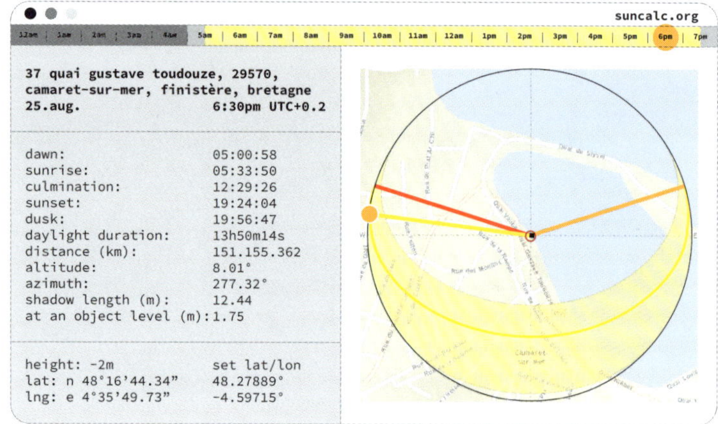

charles cottet, *evening rays, port of camaret*,
oil on canvas, 1892, 74 × 110 cm

the title, *evening rays, port of camaret*, offers precious information—it's both a timestamp and a geolocalization for the scene. thanks to the church, the building on the opposite bank, and *google street view*, we can claim that the image faces towards the east. the painter has set his easel in the west to paint the vista. the sun, which is in the west at the end of the day, is behind the artist, slightly to his left.

at this point, the last sunrays reach only the tip of the sails, the roof of the church and the last floor of a house. with many difficulties, they sill manage to overshine—but for how much longer? not much for sure—a hidden obstacle. soon, it will completely hide the setting star. but what kind of a thing would cast such an immense shadow on the sails and the buildings in the background? a u-turn on *google street view* shows us a few houses built on higher ground. were they already there at the time? the reflections of the boats on the sea surface teach us nothing. contrarily to cast shadows, they do not care for the course of the sun. when the sea is calm, reflections are equal in size to the object they mirror (but bigger if the sea grows rough).

suncalc has the last word: it is **6:30** p.m.

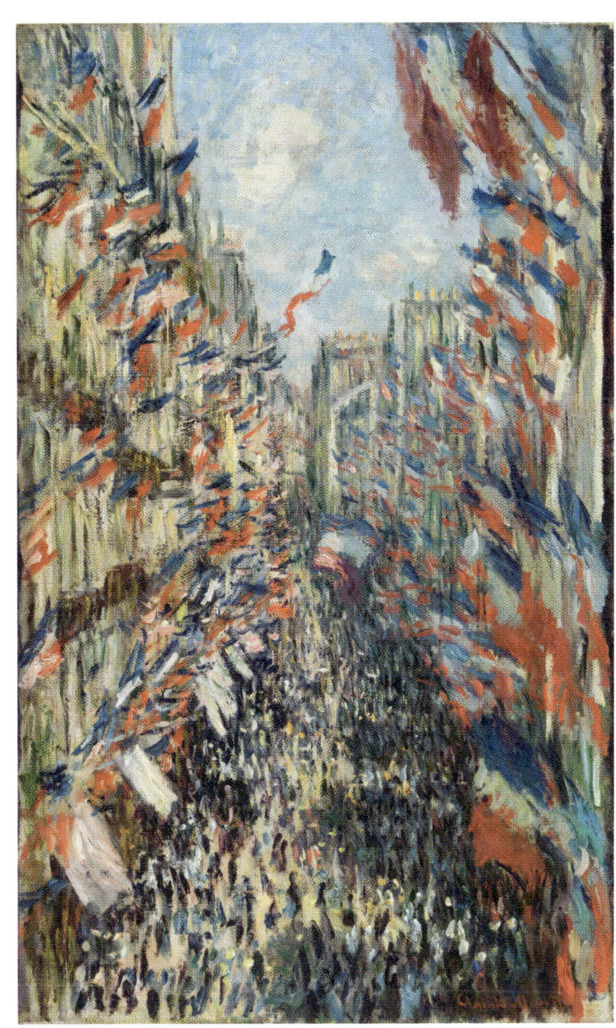

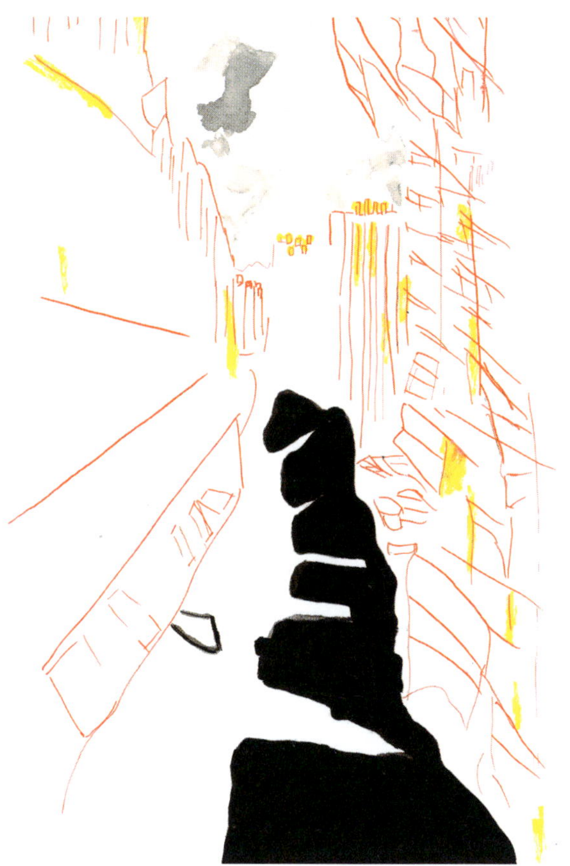

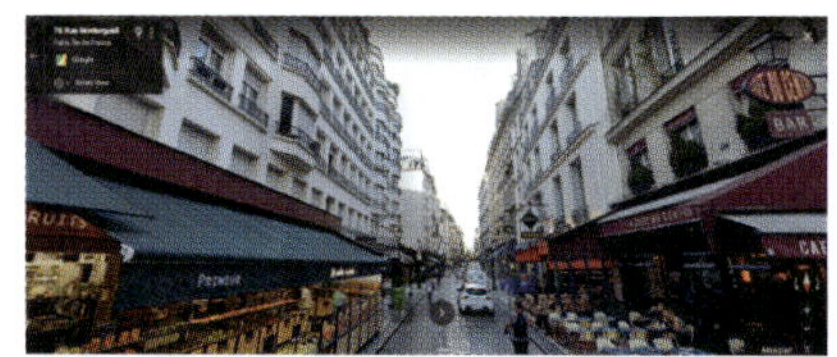

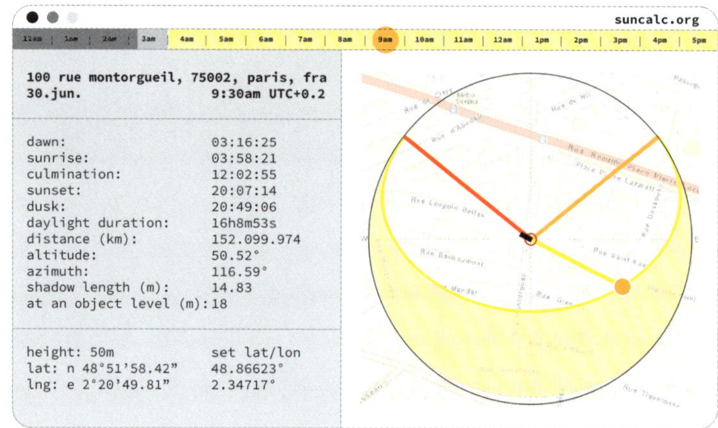

claude monet, *the rue montorgueil in paris. celebration of june 30, 1878*, oil on canvas, 1878, 81 × 50 cm

june 30, 1878. the same day, monet would make another painting, *the rue saint-denis*. according to the shadows, the sun is on the right side. the rue montorgueil, in paris, is built along a north-south axis. if we're in its southern portion, the sun is in the east; it's morning. if we're up north, the sun is in the west, it's late afternoon. if it's morning, the perspective line runs towards the rue réaumur. the shadows are not strictly perpendicular to the buildings: they point towards the north with a 20° angle. the time would be **9:30** a.m. or so. the street is 16-meter [52.49 ft.] wide, the shadows stop in the middle of it—so they are 8-meter [26.25 ft.] long. the buildings are about 6-story high, or a bit less than 20 meters [65.62 ft.] (take a height of 2.5 meters [8.20 ft.] to 3 meters [9.84 ft.] per apartment, and add the roof). the size of the shadows represents half the object casting them. but *suncalc.org* posits that, on june 30, at 9:30 a.m., a 16-meter [52.49 ft.] object should already cast a 13-meter [42.65 ft.] long shadow. for it to decrease to only 9 meters [29.53 ft.], we need to wait until **11:30** a.m. by that time, however, the shadows would have moved from the right side of the painting to become almost aligned with the north-south axis.

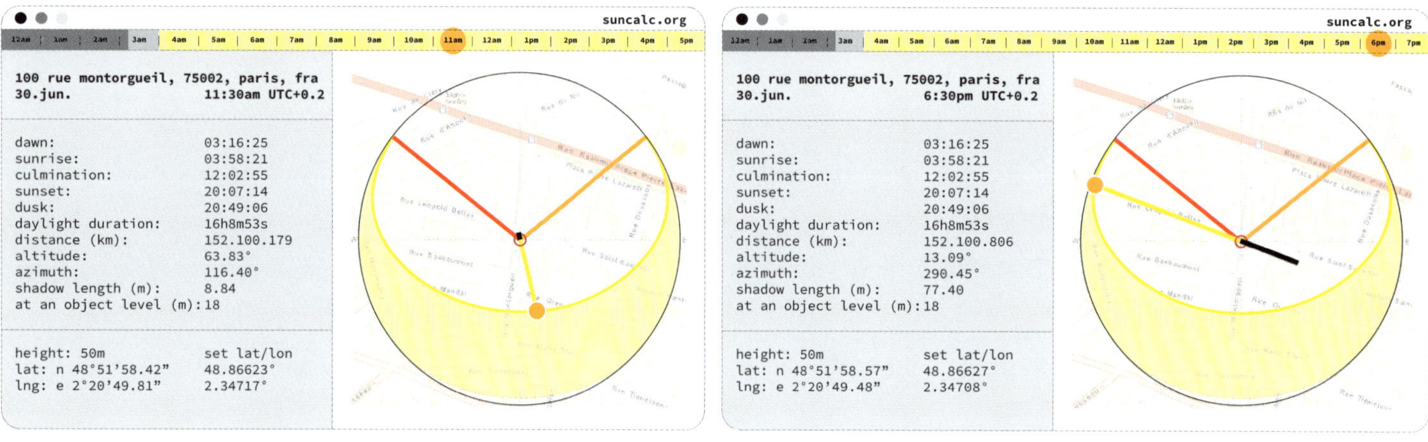
suncalc.org
12am
1am
2am
3am
4am
5am
6am
7am
8am
9am
10am
11am
12am
1pm
2pm
3pm
4pm
5pm
100 rue montorgueil, 75002, paris, fra
30.jun. 11:30am UTC+0.2
dawn: 03:16:25
sunrise: 03:58:21
culmination: 12:02:55
sunset: 20:07:14
dusk: 20:49:06
daylight duration: 16h8m53s
distance (km): 152.100.179
altitude: 63.83°
azimuth: 116.40°
shadow length (m): 8.84
at an object level (m):18
height: 50m
set lat/lon
lat: n 48°51'58.42" 48.86623°
lng: e 2°20'49.81" 2.34717°
suncalc.org
12am
1am
2am
3am
4am
5am
6am
7am
8am
9am
10am
11am
12am
1pm
2pm
3pm
4pm
5pm
6pm
7pm
100 rue montorgueil, 75002, paris, fra
30.jun. 6:30pm UTC+0.2
dawn: 03:16:25
sunrise: 03:58:21
culmination: 12:02:55
sunset: 20:07:14
dusk: 20:49:06
daylight duration: 16h8m53s
distance (km): 152.100.806
altitude: 13.09°
azimuth: 290.45°
shadow length (m): 77.40
at an object level (m):18
height: 50m
set lat/lon
lat: n 48°51'58.57" 48.86627°
lng: e 2°20'49.48" 2.34708°

monet can paint very quickly—the first painting might have been produced at the end of the afternoon. it's june, it's one of the longest days of the year. monet writes that the streets are overcrowded: "i liked the flags. during the national holiday [celebrated that year on june 30] i was strolling down rue montorgueil with my painting equipment; the street was all decked out with flags and the crowd was huge. i spot a balcony, i climb up the stairs and ask if i can paint there, they allow it. then i climb down the stairs as i came, incognito!" the sun would therefore be in the west, with monet painting in the northern portion of the street, and the line of perspective would point towards the south (and les halles neighborhood). it might be **6:30** p.m., but the buildings should cast shadows measuring up to... more than 80 meters [262.47 ft.].

so either the angle of the shadows doesn't match what monet painted (for an 8-meter [26.25 ft.] shadow, it should be 11:30 a.m., but in that case the sun would be behind his back, in the south), or the length of these shadows remains an issue (they're too long for 9:30 a.m. or 6:30 p.m.). how embarrassing... but what should we do?

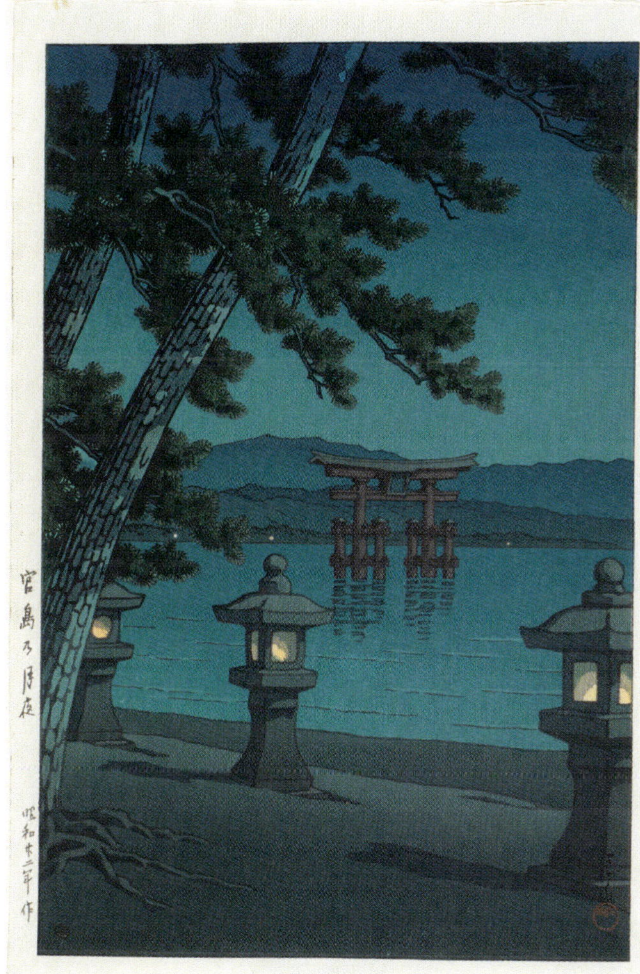
宮島の月夜
昭和十二年作

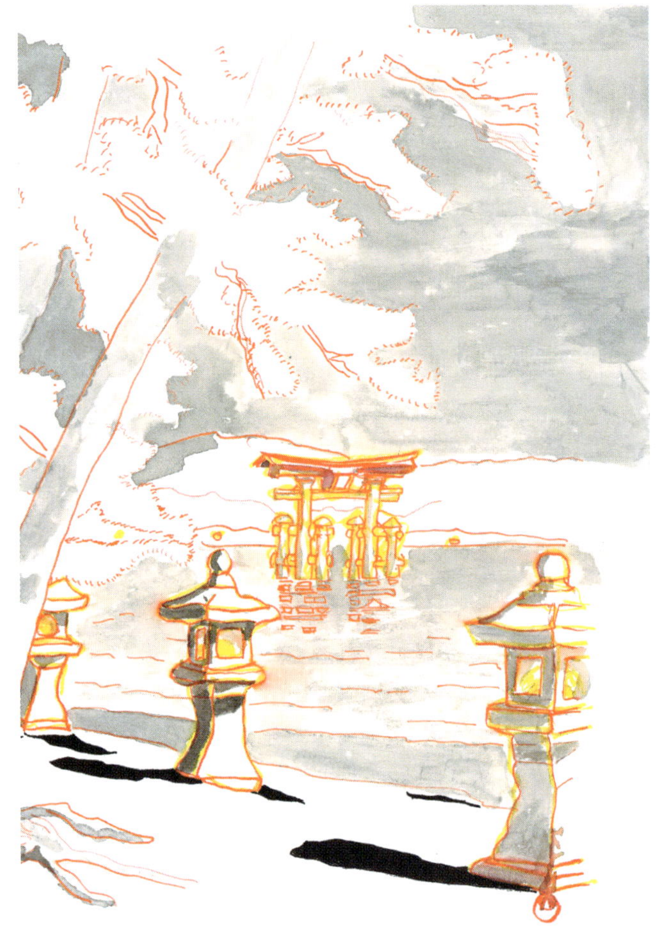

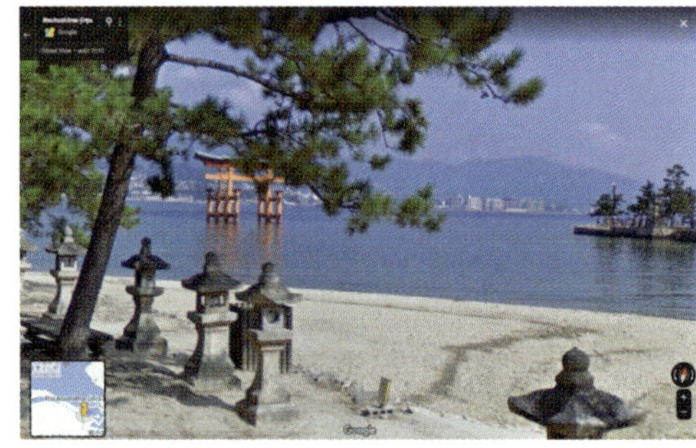

kawase hasui, ***moonlit night, miyajima***,
xylography, 1947, 38.9 × 26.3 cm

although it is night time, *google street view* effortlessly drops us off in front of the shinto shrine of itsukushima, in the hiroshima prefecture. its great vermillion-lacquered *torii* gate towers 16 meters [52.49 ft.] above the sea level and weighs more than 60 tons ; it offers one of the "three most famous views in japan" (it is also called "the gate of japan"). since its construction in 1168, only the submerged parts of the *torii* are being replaced regularly, once every century (following the *sugekae* technique). between 1947 and 2010, stone lanterns have been added, and trash cans have appeared as well, while the horizon line has welcomed several concrete buildings.

the view of the *torii* faces the north. the shadows cast by the small lanterns suggest that the moon, outside the frame, is in the east, thus beginning its ascent. the shadows cast by the lamp posts seem equal in length to them, maybe slightly shorter. although this *nihonga* exudes the feeling and atmosphere of a quiet summer night, *mooncalc.org* indicates that, for the shadows and the moon to

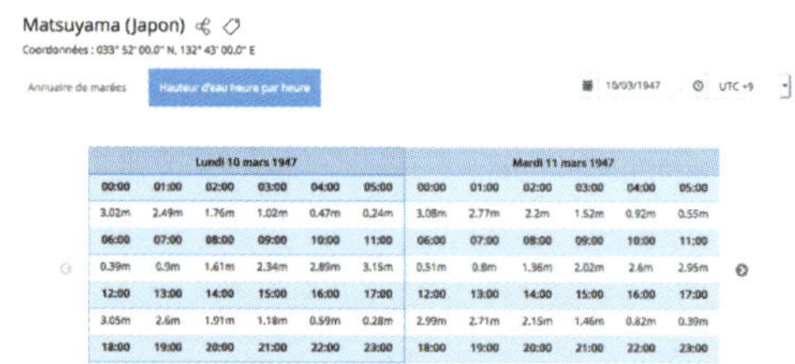

Matsuyama (Japon)

Coordonnées : 033° 52' 00.0" N, 132° 43' 00.0" E

Annuaire de marées | Hauteur d'eau heure par heure | 10/03/1947 | UTC +9

Lundi 10 mars 1947						Mardi 11 mars 1947					
00:00	01:00	02:00	03:00	04:00	05:00	00:00	01:00	02:00	03:00	04:00	05:00
3.02m	2.49m	1.76m	1.02m	0.47m	0.24m	3.08m	2.77m	2.2m	1.52m	0.92m	0.55m
06:00	07:00	08:00	09:00	10:00	11:00	06:00	07:00	08:00	09:00	10:00	11:00
0.39m	0.9m	1.61m	2.34m	2.89m	3.15m	0.51m	0.8m	1.36m	2.02m	2.6m	2.95m
12:00	13:00	14:00	15:00	16:00	17:00	12:00	13:00	14:00	15:00	16:00	17:00
3.05m	2.6m	1.91m	1.18m	0.59m	0.28m	2.99m	2.71m	2.15m	1.46m	0.82m	0.39m
18:00	19:00	20:00	21:00	22:00	23:00	18:00	19:00	20:00	21:00	22:00	23:00
0.34m	0.74m	1.39m	2.1m	2.7m	3.05m	0.28m	0.49m	0.98m	1.63m	2.25m	2.72m

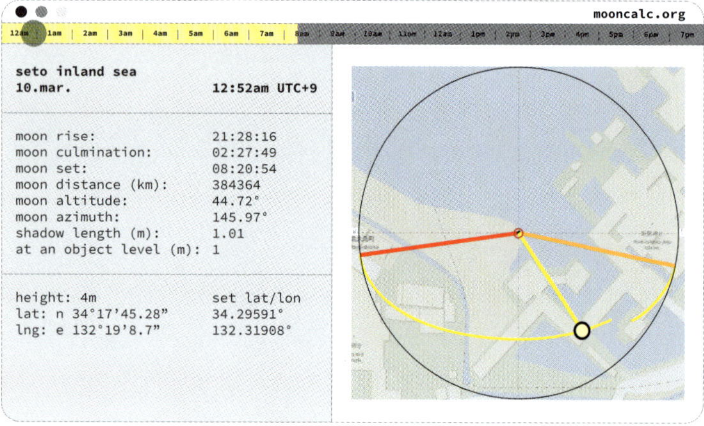

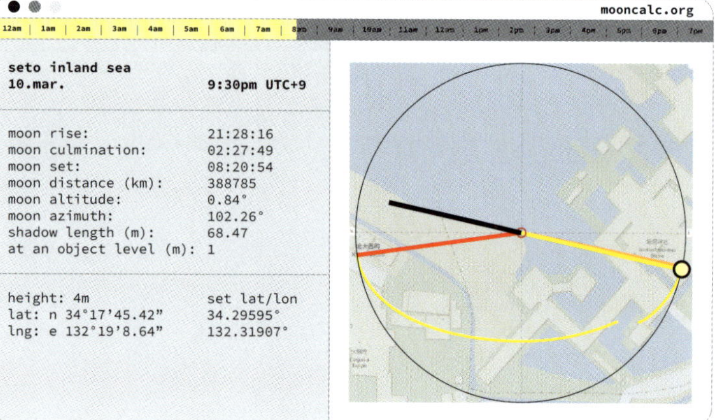

be positioned as such *at night* (for the moon can also be there *during the day*, and even in another position, also at night, but under the horizon line and therefore invisible and without shadows), the date must be march 1947, around the 10th of the month. the time would be **12:52** a.m. it's high tide, since the *torii* cannot be reached on foot, which is confirmed by *maree.shom.fr*. however, *mooncalc* also shows how everything can change because of the right-angled break in the shoreline. there is indeed a bend in the shoreline. standing a few meters before the bend would mean it is rather **3:00** a.m., but moving a few meters after it changes not only the time to **9:30** p.m. but also the length of the shadows: more than 68 meters [223.00 ft.] long for a 1-meter [3.28 ft.] high object...

kawase hasui is quite brave to come and paint the great *torii* in winter at almost 1 a.m. or is it he went there during a mild summer night, adding some shadows afterwards to give a "western" look to the artwork.

after all, wasn't that one of the goals of *nihonga* and *shin-hanga*?

generally, greek vases fall into two main categories: black-figure on red background pottery *versus* red-figure on black background pottery (which appears later). in 1898, a student of sorbonne professor edmond pottier brings to his attention the fact that many of the vases' black figures have either two left hands, or their right and left feet inverted. the professor is left speechless at first, he then considers, only to discard it, the hypothesis of poor craftmanship. finally, the student solves the riddle: if you first trace the outline of your model's shadow, and subsequently fill in the details of the limbs once the model is no longer present, it's probably very easy to inadvertently reverse left and right and therefore swap the position of the opposite limbs. conclusion: shadows were used as starting points by the greeks, when using drawing techniques, in order to preserve the original proportions (edmond pottier, *le dessin par ombre portée chez les grecs* [drawing with cast shadows in greek art], 1898).

conversation analysts, who also study body language, usually illustrate their publications with screenshots from videotaped conversations. in order to guarantee anonymity to the speakers, they cut out, using a photo editing software, all visible bodies and objects. the results are similar to some portraits by the painter gérard fromanger. smitten with such straightforward, simple, mechanical aesthetics, i tried to apply the same tool to my selection of paintings. alas, asking a software program to trace silhouettes in impressionist paintings, that by definition have no clear delineations, could only produce a glitch in the software. i had to use tracing paper to outline my objects.

in the same way that copying a text teaches us more about it than reading most comments it elicited, tracing a painting allows for a deep dive into the heart of an artist's practice. brueghel, canaletto, or renoir hence appear as documentary painters, because of myriad details, imperceptible to the naked eye, but nevertheless drawn and resolutely painted by the artists. what could appear as a conceptual gesture then connects back to copying in the most traditional sense of the activity. *learning by tracing.*

many other pieces of information besides the time of the scene depicted could be extracted from a painting. adopting police procedures could lead to precisely counting the persons present (according to the police *versus* according to the demonstrators); identifying, listing, and finding the provenance of all objects (in the manner of "*tracethisobject*"); opt for the point of view of a drone thanks to *google earth* in order to capture and recreate, from an alternative angle, a painted scene that is presented frontally (a trick the cartoonist marcel gotlib often performed with great success in his *rubriques-à-brac*). such a forensic reading would generate new metadata for the paintings, and in turn labels for museums. if labels are the artworks' *ids*, renewing the way art is described should be a major issue and challenge for art history to tackle. maybe the public of the future will decide to address and contribute to the matter? *quizchallenge* and *crowdsourcing* are already well-established tools in the intelligence community.

"like journalists covering the crucifixion"

henri michaux

credits

p13: © Mauritshuis, The Hague
p17: © Museum of Fine Arts, Boston. Gift of Quincy Adams Shaw through Quincy Adams Shaw, Jr., and Mrs. Marian Shaw Haughton, Inv. 17.1505
p21: © Virginia Museum of Fine Arts, Richmond. Collection of Mr. and Mrs. Paul Mellon, Inv. 85.498
Photo © Katherine Wetzel
p25: © KHM-Museumsverband
p29: © Colección Museo Soumaya. Fundación Carlos Slim, Ciudad de México, México
p33: © Musée d'Orsay, Dist. RMN-Grand Palais / Hervé Lewandowski
p37: © Philadelphia Museum of Art: The Henry P. McIlhenny Collection in memory of Frances P. McIlhenny, 1986, 1986-26-29
p43: © KHM-Museumsverband
p47: © Gabinetto Fotografico delle Gallerie degli Uffizi
p53: © Museo e Real Bosco di Capodimonte
p57: © Coleccion Carmen Thyssen © Museo Nacional Thyssen-Bornemisza. Madrid
p61: © National Gallery of Art, Washington
p65: © Metropolitan Museum of Art, New York
p69: © Collection of the Birmingham Museum of Art, Alabama ; Gift of the Samuel H. Kress Foundation
Photo © Sean Pathasema
p73: © The J. Paul Getty Museum, Los Angeles
p77: Royal Collection Trust © Her Majesty Queen Elizabeth II 2022
p81: © Giorgio Morara / Alamy Banque D'Images
p85: © KHM-Museumsverband
p89: © Musée d'Orsay, Dist. RMN-Grand Palais / Hervé Lewandowski
p93: © Musée d'Orsay, Dist. RMN-Grand Palais / Patrice Schmidt
p99: © Museum of Fine Arts, Boston. Gift of L. Aaron Lebowich, Inv. 50.2872

direction

David Desrimais
franck leibovici

edition

Juliette Chambon

translation

Lucas Faugère

proofreading

Cassandra Katsiaficas

graphic design

Emma Zampieri — Studio JBE

typefaces

Skolar latin (Rosetta Type)
Countach (Production Type)

photoengraving

IGS-Print

acknowledgments

Aure Bergeret
Mathieu Cénac
Didier Desrimais
Benjamin Hélion
Damien Jacq
Benjamin Lanot
Anne Leibovici
Marion Naccache
Olivia de Smedt

JBE Books
90 rue de la Folie-Méricourt
75011 Paris
jbe-books.com

ISBN: 978-2-36568-070-7
Legal deposit: January 2023

Printed in Lithuania